CASUAL
NIBBLES

ALLYSON GOFTON

CORBANS GOOD FOOD & WINE
SERIES

David Bateman

Dedication

To Rex and George for their wondrous stories, love and fabulous food, which is always
so much of an inspiration to me.

Credits

The beautiful photographs would not have been possible without the generosity of the many retailers
who allowed us endless use of their goods. Thanks to Jocelyn and her team at The Studio of Tableware,
Mt Eden; Margaux and Julie and the team at Corso Di Fiori, Newmarket; Robyn and the guys
at Indigo in Parnell; Julie and the ladies at Smith & Caugheys, Auckland; the team at
The Store in Auckland; and Jane from Trumps in Remuera.

Published in 1995 by David Bateman Ltd, Tarndale Grove, Albany Business Park,
North Shore City, Auckland, New Zealand

ISBN 1 86953 193 0

Photographs by Nick Tresidder
Printed in Hong Kong by Colorcraft Ltd

Introduction

A glass of wine and a plate of nibbles, presented casually but well, and you'll make the most of having friends in 'for drinks'; you can sit with everyone without having to get the next course going. Enjoying the company of friends is an important part of life and if you find it hard to organise parties or dinner parties, having friends in for drinks late in the afternoon is a good compromise.

There is such a fabulous selection of foods available today that the dull sandwich brigade should be long gone. I laugh when I remember the kinds of nibbles we had when I was a teenager. Edam cheese had just hit the market (big time) and a whole Edam cheese would be placed fair and square on a platter and then pierced with toothpicks studded with gherkins, pineapple pieces and cheese cubes. Remember them? They went along with cocktail sausages, sausage rolls and wine and cheese parties!

In their day these foods were exciting (amazing really), but today we can enjoy a wider range of foods from many parts of the world that not so many years ago were only read about in glossy magazines.

Our wine team has written detailed notes for this book to help you enjoy the right wine with the food you choose to prepare. Thanks for this go to Martin Carrington from Corbans Wines and Glenda Neil from *Next* magazine. Both these fabulous people have worked hard on all three books in this series and have given me lots of inspiration for recipe ideas and presentation.

A very special thank you goes to Pauline Willoughby, colleague and friend, for assisting me with the recipes and food photography for this book. Her detailed and professional work certainly cut down the stress. And thanks also to my super sister-in-law Vicki Murphy, who spent hours running around after me to help meet the deadline.

Photographer Nick Tresidder tasted his way through the book to make sure he had a good understanding of how each shot should be taken. It was his excuse, no doubt, for four weeks of overindulgence! His assistant Simon Bradley waited for the very last oyster shot before diving in as we cracked a bottle of Champagne to celebrate.

Friday nights in our home are the most casual night of the week. Warwick and I tend to sit back with a few friends, a large platter of nibbles and a bottle of wine and catch up on the week's happenings. It's a great way to wind down.

This book is a selection of my favourite ideas; some old, some new, some easy and some that need a little more time. I hope you will find something here to inspire you to take time out and relax.

Cheers!

Allyson Gofton

Contents

Potato Parmesan & Herb Fritters

Scallop Tartlets

Baby Carrot Cakes and Brandy-soaked Muffins

Crab & Ginger Wontons

Potato Blini

Antipasto Platter

Spiced New Potatoes

Rabbit with Blueberry & Cardamom Chutney

5

The Wine Cellar Guide

If you would like to begin a wine cellar, here's a guide from our team on what you need to get started.

Six bottles each of:

* High quality French Champagne, such as Taittinger, for special celebrations and gift giving.

* Good NZ Méthode Champenoise, such as Amadeus, for brunches and celebrations.

* Slightly lower-priced Chardonnay, such as Corbans Estate Gisborne, for good value drinking.

* Premium brand barrel-fermented Chardonnay, such as Corbans Private Bin Gisborne Chardonnay, for those bold seafood and white meat dishes.

* Young aggressive Sauvignon Blanc such as the classic Stoneleigh Vineyard Marlborough for all those who love wine that is best enjoyed without food.

* Oaked Sauvignon Blanc (possibly labelled Fumé Blanc) for vegetarian and other herb influenced dishes.

* Full-bodied Gewurztraminer such as Longridge of Hawkes Bay. A wine type which is vastly underrated in NZ and capable of aging extremely well. Gewurztraminer is ideal with spicy Thai and Indian foods.

* Dry Riesling such as Corbans Private Bin Amberley Rhine Riesling. Riesling has good natural acids and also tends to age extremely well. It can accompany spicy dishes but is also excellent with poultry in fruit sauces. Riesling suits a wide range of palates and tastes.

* Dessert wine, such as an extremely good botrytised Riesling. This is always a great finale to a good dinner; try it with a mature blue cheese or, for something different, as a starter with a rich pâté.

* Pinot Noir for those classic game dishes.

* Hearty Cabernet Sauvignon or Cabernet Sauvignon Merlot for barbeques and traditional roasts or casseroles.

* Light fruity red, such as a Beaujolais, ideal served chilled at picnics.

Say Cheese

Cheese is something we tend to have plenty of in our fridge, and it is one of the most versatile foods. I tend to keep expensive and special cheese to enjoy simply with crackers and bread. Others I love to cook with.

All cheese doesn't automatically go with all wines. Look out for our team's notes on wines (pages 18-19) that go with cheese, to enjoy both to the fullest.

Chilli Con Queso Dip

Hot and spicy, this Mexican dip is fabulous to serve with corn chips, crudités or other dippers.

1 tblsp oil
2-3 spring onions, minced or finely chopped
½ red pepper, minced or finely chopped
2 jalapeno peppers, minced or finely chopped
2 tsp ground cumin
1 tsp ground coriander
400-gram tin tomatoes in juice, well drained
½ x 250-gram tub cream cheese
¼ cup cream
2 cups grated tasty cheddar cheese
1½ tblsp cornflour
pepper

1 Heat the oil in a saucepan and cook the spring onions, peppers, cumin and coriander for 2-3 minutes until quite fragrant. Add the tomatoes to the saucepan and mash them down with a wooden spoon.

2 Add the cream cheese and stir until melted. Add the cream, grated cheese and cornflour. Allow to cook over a very low heat, stirring all the time, until thickened and hot. Season with pepper.

3 Serve in large bowls with corn chips, crudités or other dippers.

Makes 2 cups

Cook's Tip

Jalapeno peppers are available in the Mexican food section of most supermarkets. If you do not have them, substitute 1-2 red or green chillis. Add more or less depending on how hot you like your food.

Cheese & Sage Prawn Fritters

These are scrumptious and so easy. They are best served warm from the deep-fryer. I like using fresh breadcrumbs as they have a much better texture.

75 grams butter
¾ cup flour
2 tblsp chopped fresh sage
1½ cups milk
200 grams Gruyère cheese, diced
1 egg yolk
250 grams fresh prawns, diced

1 egg
¼ cup water or milk for crumbing
about ½ cup flour for crumbing
1 cup breadcrumbs (fresh or dried)
clean oil to deep fry

1 Heat the butter in a saucepan. Add the first measure of flour and the sage and cook for 5 minutes, stirring constantly.

2 Gradually stir in the milk to form a very thick mixture. Cook for 5 minutes. Stir in the cheese, egg yolk and prawns.

3 Turn mixture into a greased and lined 20 cm x 25 cm slab tin and refrigerate for 2-3 hours until firm.

4 Turn out and cut the mixture into squares or triangles (about 3 cm square).

5 Beat the egg and water or milk together. Dust each cheese square with flour, then dip in the egg wash and coat in breadcrumbs.

6 Deep fry in hot oil (180°C) for 3 minutes until golden and hot. Drain on absorbent paper. Serve hot with Red Pepper Mayonnaise (see page 20).

Makes about 30 small or 18 large

Pickled Asparagus & Aorangi Cheese in Filo

Aorangi is probably my favourite soft cheese. If you don't have it, substitute another soft Camembert – or try a Brie-style cheese.

340-gram bottle pickled asparagus
125 grams Aorangi cheese
12-15 sheets filo pastry
about 75 grams melted butter

1 Drain asparagus well and chop cheese roughly. In a food processor, pulse asparagus and cheese together until finely chopped but not a purée. Alternatively dice both the asparagus and cheese with a sharp knife.

2 Brush a single sheet of filo with a little melted butter. Cut the sheet in half length-wise and then fold each half on itself to form a long thin strip. Place a heaped teaspoon of mixture in the corner.

Fold filo strip over to make a triangle. Continue folding filo parcel in a triangular fashion down the length of the filo until you reach the end of the strip.

3 Place the parcel on a greased tray and brush with butter. Repeat until all filling and filo have been used up.

4 Bake at 200°C for 12-15 minutes until golden and hot. Stand for 10 minutes before serving as the cheese becomes very hot and could burn guests. Serve warm.

Makes about 3 dozen

Cook's Tips

- *If you cannot find pickled asparagus, use canned asparagus and add 1 tsp chopped green peppercorns as well.*
- *When working with filo pastry, cover all the sheets you're not using with a slightly damp cloth to prevent them drying out. I usually put a dry cloth on top and cover it with a damp cloth. Clean tea-towels are fine.*

Sables

Cheese made into delicious shortbread is one of my favourite standby nibbles. Sable is French for 'sand'; the first recipe is made with rice flour and is a bit more sandy than the second, which is more buttery in style. Keep them in airtight containers and serve them slightly warmed with drinks.

Bombay Sables

1 cup rice flour
good pinch salt
½ tsp each of ground black
    pepper, ground cumin
    and curry powder
pinch chilli powder

150 grams softened cream
    cheese
50 grams softened butter
beaten egg to glaze with
    (optional)

Topping (optional)

chilli flakes
cracked black pepper

1 Sift the flour, salt and spices into a bowl. Blend the cream cheese and butter together and then work the mixture into the sifted ingredients. Wrap in paper or plastic wrap and refrigerate for about 30 minutes.

2 Roll out the dough to 3-4 mm thick. Cut the dough out into 3-4 cm rounds and place on a well greased tray. Brush with beaten egg to glaze and top with a light dusting of chilli flakes and pepper if wished.

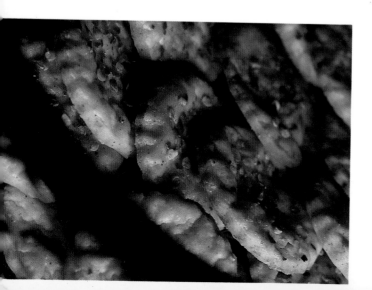

3 Bake at 170°C on fan bake or 190°C without fan for about 12 minutes, or until the sables are lightly browned on the edges and golden on top.

4 Cool on a wire rack and then store in an airtight container.

Makes about 30

Cheddar Sables

This is a very easy recipe to remember and you can make many variations on the toppings. I particularly like making them with three different coloured toppings and serving them in long lines. They go well with slices of Brie cheese.

equal quantities in weight of flour, butter and grated cheese
    (preferably a colby-style cheese; tasty cheddar seems to
    make the sables brittle)

Topping ideas

chopped pistachio nuts
sesame seeds
poppy seeds
chilli flakes (hot stuff!)
chopped walnuts or pecans
cumin or fennel seeds

1 In a bowl, sift the flour. Grate the butter and work into the flour with the cheese until the mixture forms a firm dough.

2 Turn out the mixture and bring together. Roll out on a floured board to about 3-4 mm thick and cut into rounds or shapes.

3 Place on a greased baking tray and sprinkle over your preferred topping.

4 Bake at 200°C for about 12-15 minutes until the biscuits are golden. Transfer while hot to a cake rack to cool and then store in an airtight container.

Makes about 30

Parmesan Pita Toasts

Hot from under the grill, these are sensational – so our photographer Nick Tresidder thought, as he proceeded to devour all the ones on this lovely plate!

1 packet large pita bread pockets (5 pockets)
½ cup virgin olive oil
4 tblsp finely grated Parmesan cheese
2 tsp lemon pepper
2 tblsp sesame seeds

1 Split each piece of pita bread in two. Cut each piece into 8 wedges.

2 Combine olive oil, Parmesan cheese, lemon pepper and sesame seeds.

3 Using a pastry brush, brush a little of the cheese mixture onto the cut side (inside) of each wedge of bread.

4 Place on baking tray. Grill under a medium heat until crunchy and golden brown.

5 Store in an airtight container. Warm before serving.

Makes 80 wedges

Double Cream Cheese Fritters with Plum Sauce

Loaded with cheese, these fritters are particularly delicious with a light fruity homemade fresh plum sauce. I like Whitestone or Kapiti cheeses in this recipe.

1 tsp dry yeast
¾ cup warm milk
25 grams butter, melted
1 tsp sugar
3 rashers bacon
1½ cups flour
1 tsp salt

2 tblsp chopped fresh
    oregano
1 egg
200 grams double cream
    soft cheese (Brie style),
    finely diced

1 Put the yeast, warm milk, melted butter and sugar into a bowl, stir well and set aside in a warm place for about 10 minutes until the yeast is lovely and frothy.

2 Cut and discard the rind from the bacon. Cook the bacon in a frying pan until it is crispy. Drain on absorbent paper.

3 Sift the flour and salt into a large bowl. Stir in the herbs and bacon and make a well in the centre. Beat the egg lightly and stir into the yeast mixture. Pour into the well with the diced cheese. Mix together well with a wooden spoon or use your hand. Beat for 2 minutes.

4 Cover with greased plastic wrap and set aside in a warm place until the mixture has doubled in bulk. Do not knock down once risen.

5 Deep-fry spoonfuls of the dough at 180°C for about 4 minutes until the balls rise to the top of the oil and are golden brown. Drain well on absorbent paper and keep warm in the oven.

6 Serve with the plum sauce.

Makes about 30

Plum Sauce

This recipe comes from Pauline Willoughby, who worked with me preparing the food and photography in this book. Spicy plum sauce is one of her favourite accompaniments for cheese, and this one is not too sharp. You will need ripe red plums for this.

500 grams red plums, stoned
½ cup water
¾ cup sugar
¼ cup spiced or cider vinegar

1 Place the plums, water, sugar and vinegar into a saucepan and simmer gently for about 15 minutes until the plums have softened.

2 Purée in a food processor and then sieve to remove the skins.

Makes approx 1 1/2 cups

Cook's Tip

The balls can be warmed up in the oven for about 10 minutes at 180°C in a single layer if you have made them in advance.

Marinated Olives in Cheat's Cheese Pastry

These darling-looking nibbles are indeed a mere mouthful of flavour. You can make them in no time using purchased goods.

2 sheets Ernest Adams savoury pastry
¼ cup finely grated Parmesan cheese
32 large marinated and stoned black olives

1 Sprinkle each sheet of pastry with 2 tblsp Parmesan cheese. Roll lightly so cheese is pressed into the pastry. Cut each square of pastry into 16 equal smaller squares.

2 To wrap each olive, turn the square of pastry over so the Parmesan is on the outside. Place olive in centre and bring the four corners together, and squeeze.

3 Place on oven tray. Bake at 190°C for 15-20 minutes or until pastry is golden brown. Serve warm.

Makes 32

Variations

Use jumbo green stuffed olives or smaller marinated olives and cut pastry into 4-cm squares.

Hushpuppies with Fresh Tomato Dip

From way down south in Louisiana, hush-puppies are made from a cornbread mix. The story goes that in order to keep the dogs quiet on the farm, balls of cornbread mix were deep-fried and thrown out to the howling hounds with a shout of 'hush puppies!'. It's a great story, even if you're sceptical. Enjoy them with a chunky fresh tomato dip.

1 cup flour
¾ cup fine cornmeal
2 tsp baking powder
salt and pepper
2 tsp ground coriander
¼ tsp chilli powder

2 spring onions, trimmed
  and finely chopped
1 egg
¾ cup milk
oil for deep frying

1 Sift flour, cornmeal, baking powder, salt, pepper, coriander and chilli powder into a bowl. Stir in the spring onions.

2 Lightly beat egg and milk together and pour into the dry ingredients. Mix to form a smooth batter.

3 Drop small teaspoonfuls into hot oil and deep-fry at 180°C until puffed up and golden brown. Drain on paper towels. Serve hot with fresh tomato dip.

Makes about 40

Variations

Add chopped ham, jalapeno peppers, corn kernels or diced cheese to the mixture if wished.

Fresh Tomato Dip

Tomatoes are a big part of the food of Louisiana. Here I have puréed fresh tomatoes with Tabasco sauce and basil for a simple fresh dip to enjoy with the hushpuppies.

2 large beef steak
  tomatoes, blanched and
  peeled
½ stick celery
1 spring onion
¼ small cucumber

¼ cup tomato purée
good dash Tabasco Sauce
2-3 tblsp chopped fresh
  basil
freshly ground black
  pepper

1 Roughly chop the tomatoes, celery and spring onions. Peel cucumber and remove the seeds. *To do this, peel the cucumber then use a teaspoon to run down the centre of the cucumber to lift up all the seeds easily and quickly.*

2 In a food processor or blender, process the chopped vegetables, tomato purée, Tabasco Sauce and basil until almost smooth. Season well with pepper.

3 Serve chilled.

Makes 1 cup

Baby Crab, Gruyère & Lemon Grass Tartlets

This sounds like an odd collection of foods snuggled into a tartlet, but the flavours work well together.

1 stalk lemon grass
25 grams butter
2 spring onions, trimmed
*   and finely sliced*
3 eggs
¾ cup cream

½ tsp ground black pepper
170-gram can crabmeat,
*   well drained*
100 grams Gruyère
*   cheese, grated*
24-28 baby pastry cases

1 Trim the lemon grass where it becomes green. Discard the stringy green reed and finely slice the white bulb end. Heat the butter in a saucepan and cook the spring onions and lemon grass for about 5 minutes. Set aside.

2 Lightly beat eggs, cream and black pepper together.

3 Combine egg mixture, spring onions, crabmeat and cheese.

4 Spoon crab mixture into pastry cases. Bake at 190°C for 12-15 minutes or until cooked and golden.

M a k e s   2 4 - 2 8

Frittata with Kumara, Roasted Pepper & Thyme

These frittata nibbles can be made in advance, then cut into chunky slices and decorated just before serving.

1 large red pepper
1 tblsp olive oil
1 small onion, peeled and diced
400 grams kumara
8 eggs

½ cup cream
1 cup grated Edam or Gouda cheese
salt and pepper
¼ cup chopped fresh thyme, oregano and parsley

To garnish

créme fraîche or sour cream
fresh thyme
sliced sun-dried red peppers or tomatoes in oil
caper berries

1 Grill the red pepper under a hot grill until blackened all over. Place in plastic bag or container until cool. Core, remove seeds and peel away charred skin under cold running water. Dry on a paper towel and slice finely.

2 Heat the olive oil in medium-sized frying pan (about 20 cm diameter). Cook onion and kumara over a moderate heat until they are just beginning to brown. Add red pepper.

3 Lightly beat eggs, cream and grated cheese together. Season with salt, pepper, thyme, oregano and parsley, and pour over the kumara slices in the hot pan.

4 Cook over low to medium heat until egg has set. Remove from the heat and allow to cool. Serve cut into squares with a little sour cream or crème fraîche, a herb garnish, and slices of red peppers or tomatoes on top. Try deep-fried caper berries on the side to garnish.

Variations

- Potatoes, red pepper and black olives.

- Courgettes, yellow pepper and salami.

- Mushrooms, bacon and sun-dried tomatoes.

- Smoked fish, tomato and green olives.

- Courgettes, cubed blue cheese and pinenuts.

Cook's Tip

If you can get it, fresh crabmeat makes these a little more special. If you cannot find canned crabmeat, use minced fresh prawns or shrimps.

Crushed Goat's Cheese in Filo with an Apricot & Curry Dipper

This is a feta lover's delight. If you are not fond of this tangy cheese, you could use Edam, a Brie-style cheese or even a smoked cheese.

400 grams feta cheese
¼ cup toasted desiccated coconut
20 sheets filo pastry
100 grams butter, melted

Apricot and Curry Dipper

1 tblsp butter
1 small onion, peeled and sliced
2 tsp curry powder
400-gram tin unsweetened apricots
½ cup coconut milk

1 Cut feta into about 40 long thin pieces, each about 6 cm long. Roll the feta sticks in coconut.

2 Cut filo pastry sheets into half lengthwise. Brush filo sheet with butter and fold in half cross-wise. Place feta cheese on pastry and tuck in the sides. Roll up to enclose the feta. Place on a greased baking tray. Repeat using all cheese and pastry. Brush the parcels with butter.

3 Bake at 190°C for 15 minutes or until golden brown. Serve warm or cold with Apricot and Curry Dipper.

Makes 40

Apricot and Curry Dipper

Heat the butter in a saucepan and cook onion until soft. Add curry powder and cook a further 2 minutes. Place onion, apricots (including juice) and coconut milk in food processor and process until smooth.

Cook's Tip

Toast coconut in a 180°C oven for 10-12 minutes until browned. Alternatively, you can toss the coconut in a pan over a moderate heat until golden.

17

Cashew & Camembert Pâté

¾ cup raw cashew nuts, roasted and cooled
250 grams large Camembert or Brie, at room temperature
¼ cup finely chopped or minced dried apricots
¼ cup cream cheese
1 tblsp chopped chives

1 Chop cashews roughly and set 3 tblsp aside for garnish.

2 Using a sharp knife, cut a thin top off the Camembert or Brie and discard the rind.

3 Using a teaspoon, scoop out the soft cheese from the rind and place in a small bowl. Mix in the cashew nuts, apricots, cream cheese and chives. Stir until mixture is soft and creamy.

4 Spoon the mixture back into the empty shell. Sprinkle the reserved cashew nuts on top.

5 Serve at room temperature with crackers.

Variations

- Use 2 small (125 grams) cheeses instead.

- In place of apricots try dried peaches, mango or pineapple.

Ricotta & Gherkin Pâté

A quick soft cheese spread, ideal for salty style crackers.

¾ cup grated very tasty
   Cheddar cheese
¾ cup ricotta cheese
½ cup cream cheese
1 spring onion, trimmed
   and finely chopped

¼ cup chopped gherkins
1 tblsp Worcestershire sauce
½ cup chopped parsley
   (preferably Italian)
½ cup chopped walnuts,
   slightly toasted

Wine & Cheese

Wine and cheese have always been considered to be perfect partners. But what is the secret behind this successful relationship? Firstly, wine is acid and cheese is alkaline, so they are always going to be contrasting, rather than complementary. Also, cheese tends to coat the palate and wine clears it.

Finding combinations that work is really a matter of trial and error; there are no hard-and-fast rules. The more you experiment with various flavours and textures of wine and cheese, the more likely you are to find surprising and delicious matches.

I have divided the cheeses into groupings and made wine suggestions that I found good, but don't be afraid to try combinations other than these, the possibilities are unlimited as there are so many different wine and cheese styles available.

Young Cheddar – Mild Cheddar, Colby & Swiss style – Edam, Gouda, Gruyère, Elsberg

These cheeses match well with soft, fruity red wines or a buttery Chardonnay. Try Longridge of Hawkes Bay Cabernet Sauvignon Merlot or

1 In a bowl blend together the grated cheese, ricotta cheese, cream cheese, spring onion, gherkins, Worcestershire sauce, half the parsley and half the walnuts to make a well-blended mix.

2 Spread into a serving bowl and then sprinkle over the remaining walnuts and parsley and refrigerate for about 1 hour before serving.

3 Serve with crackers.

Makes about 2 1/2 cups

Robard & Butler South East Australian Cabernet Shiraz. An ideal white accompaniment would be Stoneleigh Vineyard Marlborough Chardonnay.

Aged Cheddar – Tasty, Vintage

A Gewurztraminer, such as the Robard & Butler Marlborough Gewurztraminer or Longridge of Hawkes Bay Gewurztraminer. Or try a bold red, such as a Stoneleigh Vineyard Marlborough Cabernet Sauvignon or Robard & Butler South East Australian Shiraz.

Brine Ripened – Feta, Mozzarella, Bocconcini

Pinot Noir, such as the Cottage Block Pinot Noir, would be ideal. Or opt for an oak-aged Sauvignon Blanc such as the Longridge of Hawkes Bay Oak Aged Sauvignon Blanc or Corbans Private Bin Wood Aged Sauvignon Blanc.

Fresh Cheese – Ricotta, Cottage, Marscapone, Quark

The very delicate flavours of these cheeses are easily overpowered by wine. Try a delicate style like a young Müller Thurgau, such as Corbans White Label or Waimanu.

White Mould Ripened (Young) – Brie, Camembert

Enjoy with a Chardonnay; look for a Gisborne Chardonnay from Corbans White Label or Corbans Private Bin. Méthode Champenoise

– such as Champernay or Amadeus – is a good choice for these cheeses too. You could also try a Longridge of Hawkes Bay Cabernet Sauvignon Merlot for a well-flavoured red with sweet, ripe fruit.

Sheep & Goats Cheese – Hipi Iti, Chevre

Try with a dry Riesling, such as the Corbans Private Bin Amberley Rhine Riesling or Corbans White Label Johannisberg Riesling. Sauvignon Blanc is another excellent match – try one from Stoneleigh Vineyard Marlborough or Corbans White Label.

Hard Cheese – Parmesan, Romano

A light, fruity, dry finish red wine or a dry Riesling will work best with these styles. For red wines try the Hawkes Bay Cabernet Sauvignon or the South East Australian Shiraz. Two Rieslings to try are the Corbans White Label Johannisberg and the Corbans Private Bin Amberley Rhine Riesling.

Blue Mould Ripened – Blue Vein, Blue Supreme, Blue de Bresse, Blue Brie

Sweet dessert wines are a great match with blue cheeses, as are Tawny Port, like the Robard & Butler Tawny Port or Cellarmans Tawny Port, and red wines with good ripe fruit and weight. Gewurztraminer also makes a stunning match with blue Brie; try the Longridge of Hawkes Bay Gewurztraminer or the Robard & Butler.

1 packet Continental Potato Patties
    with Cheese and Onion
1¼ cups boiling water
¼ cup Parmesan cheese
¼ cup chopped chives
¼ cup chopped parsley
2 tblsp flour
clean oil to deep-fry

1 Place contents of both the sachets in the packet into a bowl. Add boiling water and stir well. Allow to stand for 8 minutes.

2 Add Parmesan cheese and herbs.

3 Shape into walnut-size balls and roll in flour. Deep-fry 2-3 minutes or until golden brown. Drain on absorbent paper before serving.

4 Serve with Red Pepper Mayonnaise

Makes 30

Potato, Parmesan & Herb Fritters with Red Pepper Mayonnaise

These tiny morsels are made quickly using a packet mix and they taste great. Keep a packet of the Continental Potato mix on hand to en-sure you can whip these up any time!

Red Pepper Mayonnaise

1 Grill 1 red pepper until blackened all over. Place in a freezer bag or in a plastic container and allow to cool. When cool, peel away the charred skin under cold running water and discard the seeds and core.

2 Purée the red pepper in a blender with 2 cloves peeled garlic. Mix in 1 cup thick homemade mayonnaise and purée to blend. Season with a good dash of lemon juice.

Sweet Thoughts

If you are planning coffee after a few drinks, it is nice to have something delicious on hand to enjoy at the end of a great evening. My favourites include the Chestnut and Chocolate Truffles; and for ease of preparation the Black and White Amaretti Biscuits cannot be beaten.

Fudgey Nut Slice

This is rich and decadent – enjoy it cut into thick slices. It's great to serve at special celebration nibbles.

1 sheet pre-rolled Ernest
    Adams butter pastry
2 x 70-gram packet
    hazelnuts
70-gram packet pecans
    or walnuts
125 grams unsalted butter
¾ cup firmly packed
    brown sugar
½ cup cream
grated rind 1 lemon
    or orange
2 tblsp lemon juice
2 eggs
½ cup flour

Topping

2 x 70-gram packet nuts
    (use walnuts, Brazil nuts or pecans)
3 tblsp apricot jam

1 Roll out the pastry and use it to line the base and sides of an oblong slice tin (tranche tin). The size is approximately 34 cm x 10 cm. Bake blind at 190°C for 12-15 minutes or until the pastry is cooked.

2 Roast the first three packets of nuts in a 180°C oven for 10-12 minutes, until the nuts are beginning to brown. Cool and chop roughly.

3 Melt the butter and brown sugar in a saucepan. Add the cream, nuts, lemon or orange rind and lemon juice. Remove from the heat and beat in the eggs and sifted flour. Pour into the prepared tin.

4 Sprinkle over the packets of nuts for the topping. Bake at 180°C for 30 minutes, or until the filling is set.

5 Brush the slice with the warmed apricot jam while it is still hot. Cool and serve in slices.

Makes 12-16 slices

Wine suggestions

Wine with sweet foods can be a difficult match, especially with those that include chocolate and lots of lemon (see the section on simple wine and food matching, pages 70-71). The best matches for sweet foods are dessert wines, ports, muscat or sweeter bubblies, such as Diva.

Cook's Tip

Remember to keep nuts in the freezer. Nuts have a high oil content and they will go rancid if left in a warm pantry cupboard.

Ann's Baby Carrot Cakes

This is an adaptation of a cake recipe given to me by a super friend in Launceston, Tasmania. Ann makes this cake regularly for her family. I have changed it into little muffins, decorated with the traditional but ever-so-yummy icing, and served them up as tiny mouthful-sized morsels, ideal for enjoying at the end of the evening.

1 cup flour
1 tsp baking powder
½ cup sugar
1 cup finely grated carrot
½ cup canned peach filling
125 grams butter, melted
½ cup milk
2 eggs

Icing

125 grams cream cheese
1 tblsp each icing sugar, runny honey and milk
2 oranges for garnishing

1 Sift the flour, baking powder and sugar into a large bowl. Stir through the finely grated carrot and make a well in the centre.

2 In another bowl, blend together the peaches, butter, milk and eggs. Pour into the well and stir gently to mix.

3 Three-quarters fill 24-30 greased baby muffin tins. Bake at 220°C for about 10-12 minutes until golden and cooked.

4 Allow to stand in the tins for a few minutes before transferring to a wire rack to cool. Ice, then use a citrus zester to make strips of orange zest and place some of these fine shreds on top of the muffins before serving.

Makes 24-30

Icing

In a bowl, blend together the cream cheese, icing sugar, honey and milk. Taste for sweetness, as you may like to add a little bit more icing sugar or honey.

Hot Brandy-Soaked Muffins

Made with ease, they are ideal to have with drinks at Christmas time.

2 cups self-raising flour
½ cup caster sugar
100 grams butter
2 eggs
1 cup milk
1¼ cups raisins in Brandy Syrup (see page 23)

1 Sift the flour into a large bowl. Stir in the sugar and make a well in the centre.

2 Melt the butter. Add the eggs and milk and mix together well.

3 Pour the liquid ingredients and the raisins into the well and stir lightly with a holed spoon until the mixture is combined.

4 Spoon the mixture into 12 well greased muffin tins. Bake at 200°C for 10-12 minutes until golden and cooked.

5 Serve warm dusted with icing sugar.

Makes 12 large or 36 small muffins

Chestnut & Chocolate Truffles

These little morsels hail from Spain and are particularly nice to enjoy with a rich-tasting coffee.

250 grams cooking
   chocolate
75 grams unsalted butter
435-gram can chestnut
   purée

½ cup caster sugar
2 tblsp brandy
70-gram packet ground
   almonds

1 Chop the chocolate roughly and place into a bowl with the butter. Melt over a saucepan of simmering hot water. Remove and allow to cool.

2 Sieve or beat the chestnut purée until smooth. Add the purée, sugar and brandy to the chocolate mixture. Refrigerate until the mixture has become cold.

3 Roll teaspoonfuls into balls and toss in the ground almonds. Place in small truffle cases and keep in an airtight container in the refrigerator.

Makes about 40

Cook's Tip

These truffles will not go hard, but remain slightly soft.

Raisins in Brandy Syrup

These are an ideal gift, and can be used as an accompaniment to ice-cream or rich chocolate cake. If you can get hold of them, muscatel raisins are the best for this recipe.

500 grams muscatel raisins
½ cup water
½ cup sugar

¼ cup brandy
2 vanilla pods

1 Put the raisins, water, sugar and brandy in a saucepan. Bring to a slow simmer, stirring until the sugar has dissolved. Add the vanilla pods.

2 Simmer gently for 5-10 minutes, until the raisins have soaked up most of the syrup. Bottle into a hot sterilized jar and seal.

Makes approx 2 cups

Variation

- Use other liqueurs or spirits in place of brandy: whisky or Grand Marnier would be nice.

Chocolate Pretzels

These chocolate-coated shortbreads are great to have with coffee or to add to a platter of sweet ideas.

3 tblsp Kahlua
2 tblsp hot water
¼ cup cocoa
175 grams butter
½ cup caster sugar
2 eggs

1 tsp vanilla essence
3 cups flour
1 tsp ground ginger
200 grams cooking
    chocolate
1 tblsp Kremelta

1 Heat the Kahlua and water together and stir in the cocoa to dissolve it. Set aside to cool.

2 Beat the butter and sugar together until the mixture is light and creamy. Add the eggs and vanilla, and beat well.

3 Sift the flour and ginger together. Stir into the creamed mixture with the dissolved cocoa mixture. Turn out onto a floured board and bring together. Wrap in plastic wrap and refrigerate for about 1 hour.

4 Roll small amounts of about 1 tablespoon out to 18-cm lengths. Place your wrist on the bench and take hold of each end of the dough. Bring the ends up, crossing them over and pressing them on the back of the dough to form a pretzel that looks like those in the picture. Place them on a greased baking tray. Repeat with remaining mixture.

5 Bake at 190°C for about 15 minutes until cooked. Cool on a wire rack.

6 Roughly chop the chocolate and melt with the Kremelta in a double saucepan over a simmering water bath. This can be done in the microwave but be careful as chocolate burns easily.

7 Dip the top of each pretzel in the melted chocolate. Place on a cake rack to cool and set. Store in an airtight container.

Makes 36-40

Black & White Amaretti

Amaretti biscuits are interesting macaroon-like treats you can purchase pre-made. They are intensely almond flavoured and go well dipped in chocolate. Prepared with bought biscuits, this is an ideal recipe for busy people.

75 grams dark chocolate
about 40 Amaretti biscuits (2 packets)
75 grams white chocolate

1 Melt the dark chocolate in a small dish over simmering water, or in microwave on low for 1 minute.

2 Dip almost half of each biscuit in dark chocolate. Set aside for the chocolate to become hard (a cake cooling rack is good to use for this).

3 Melt white chocolate as above. Dip the other side of each biscuit in white chocolate (leaving a narrow strip of biscuit showing between the dark and white chocolate). Set aside.

4 Use any leftover chocolate to pipe decoratively on top (see photo opposite).

5 Store in an airtight container.

Makes 40

Bitter Sables

These are rich, buttery little morsels that are super to have on hand. If you are not a lover of Angostura Bitters, use an alcohol that you prefer. Angostura gives this shortbread-style biscuit a superb flavour.

300 grams butter
1/2 cup caster sugar
1 egg yolk
1 tblsp Angostura Bitters
2 cups flour

1/2 tsp salt
1/2 tsp baking powder
2 x 70-gram packets whole
    blanched almonds

1 Beat the butter and sugar together until they are very light and creamy. Allow about 8-10 minutes to ensure the mixture is very light.

2 Beat in the egg yolk and Angostura Bitters.

3 Sift the flour, salt and baking powder together and stir into the creamed mixture. Turn out onto a floured board and bring the mixture together. Wrap up in plastic wrap and then refrigerate for about 1 hour.

4 Roll out on a floured board to about 0.5 cm thickness. Cut into shapes and place on a greased baking tray. Place a whole almond on each biscuit.

5 Bake at 180°C for about 10 minutes until they are lightly golden.

6 Cool on a cake rack and store in an airtight container.

Makes about 36

Marzipan Shorts

These are incredibly almondy-tasting morsels; super to accompany a liqueur coffee.

3/4 cup castor sugar
200 grams butter
150 grams softened
    marzipan

few drops almond essence
2 cups flour
1 1/2 tsp baking powder
1/4 cup ground almonds

1 Beat the caster sugar and butter together in a large bowl until light and creamy. Beat in the marzipan and almond essence.

2 Sift the flour and baking powder together and stir into the creamed mixture with the ground almonds.

3 Place small dessertspoonfuls of mixture onto greased baking trays. Bake at 180°C for about 15 minutes until they are firm to the touch and lightly browned. Cool on a wire rack.

4 Store in an airtight container and then dust well with icing sugar when serving.

Makes about 36

Cook's Tips

- *These are nice if they have been warmed slightly before they are dusted with the icing sugar to serve.*
- *Use Odense marzipan or another good brand. Do not use almond-flavoured icing as this will dissolve when cooling and cause the biscuits to fail.*

Cook's Tip

You can make the biscuit mixture one or two days ahead if you wish. Keep well wrapped in the refrigerator and allow 1 hour at room temperature before rolling out.

Sweet Cherry Pastries

Short buttery pastry filled with a sweet dried fruit mixture makes for great nibbles.

¾ cup milk

¼ cup semolina

2 tblsp sugar

1 egg

3 sheets Ernest Adams Pre-rolled Butter Crust Pastry

¼ cup dried fruit (½ mixed peel and ½ chopped cherries, or any other combination of dried fruit)

¼ cup ricotta cheese

1 Heat milk to simmering point. Add semolina gradually while stirring constantly with a wooden spoon. Continue cooking on low while stirring for about 5 minutes, or until mixture is very thick.

2 Remove from heat and stir in the sugar, egg and dried fruit. Mix well.

3 Sieve or purée ricotta cheese and stir in. Set mixture aside until cold.

4 Roll pastry sheets to make the pastry a little thinner. Cut into circles 7 cm across.

5 Place a little of the filling mixture in the middle of each circle. Fold over and press edges together with a fork.

6 Bake at 180°C for 15-20 minutes, or until just beginning to go light brown.

7 Serve warm or cold sprinkled with icing sugar.

Makes about 36

Cook's Tip

In a cooking shop in the United States I found a little tartlet maker, a gadget which is hinged in the centre. You put the pastry round on top, a teaspoon of filling in the centre and then you flip over one side and squeeze, joining both sides together to make a mini pastie. You can find them here, so look out for them.

Chocolate Nut Slice

This is always a great standby to keep on hand. Toasting the nuts is essential to achieve a rich flavour.

70-gram packet each of hazelnuts, Brazil nuts and blanched almonds
250 grams cooking chocolate

½ x 400-gram tin sweetened condensed milk
1 tblsp brandy

1 Place hazelnuts, Brazil nuts and almonds on a baking tray and cook 10 minutes until lightly toasted. Allow to cool.

2 Melt chocolate in a bowl over simmering water. Remove from heat and stir in condensed milk, nuts and brandy.

3 Line a 25 cm x 8 cm slice tin with tin foil. Spread mixture into tin and refrigerate.

4 To serve, remove from tin, peel away foil and cut into wafer-thin slices.

Cook's Tips

- *This slice will keep in the refrigerator for up to two weeks.*
- *If you do not have a bar tin, use a small loaf tin and cut each slice in half.*
- *Try other nuts such as pecans, walnuts or cashew nuts. Nuts may be roughly chopped instead of left whole.*

Fudgey Banana Cakes with Caramel Dipping Sauce

These small cakes are solid banana, with a decadent dipping sauce to turn them into something special. You can make these in advance and warm them as needed.

2 large bananas
1 tblsp golden syrup
1 tsp vanilla
2 eggs
1½ cups flour
1 tsp baking powder
½ tsp baking soda
½ cup caster sugar
150 grams butter, melted
70-gram packet pecans, toasted

Caramel Dipping Sauce

100 grams butter
½ cup brown sugar
¾ cup double cream
icing sugar

1 In a food processor, put the bananas, golden syrup, vanilla essence and eggs, and process until smooth.

2 In a large mixing bowl, sift the flour, baking powder, baking soda and caster sugar. Make a well in the centre and pour in the melted butter and the banana mixture. Use a holed spoon to mix together.

3 Three-quarters fill 36 small greased muffin tins and decorate each with half a pecan. Bake at 220°C for 12 minutes, or until the muffins are cooked. Cool in the tin for about 2-3 minutes before transferring to a cake rack to cool.

4 Dust with icing sugar and serve with the dipping sauce.

Makes 36

Caramel Dipping Sauce

Put the butter and sugar into a microwave-proof glass bowl and cook on 100% power for 3 minutes. Stir in the cream and cook a further 2 minutes. If you do not have a microwave, cook in a saucepan, but stir constantly to prevent burning.

From the East

Spicy foods, fragrant with ginger, garlic, soy, coriander, peppers and curry, make up the ideas in this chapter. Matching the right wines to go with this style of food is important – our team offers lots of ideas and tips for happy combinations.

Chilli Beef on Prawn Crackers

Hot, sweet and sour all in a cracker.

2 tblsp oil	250 grams minced beef
2 cloves garlic, peeled and crushed	2 kaffir lime leaves
1 tblsp finely chopped root ginger	½ cup beef stock
	1 tsp cornflour
1 tsp laos powder	1 tsp nam pla
¼ tsp each ground chilli powder, nutmeg and ground coriander	2 tblsp sherry
	2 spring onions, trimmed and finely chopped
good shake of ground cloves	about 30 prawn crackers
1 tsp grated lemon rind	oil for deep-frying

1 Heat oil in a frying pan and cook garlic and ginger over a low heat for about 3 minutes until fragrant. Add laos powder, chilli, nutmeg, coriander, cloves and lemon rind and cook a further 2-3 minutes.

2 Add minced beef and break up with a fork and brown. Stir in kaffir lime leaves and stock, and simmer for 10 minutes.

3 Mix cornflour to a paste with nam pla and sherry and stir into beef. Cook only until thickened. Stir in the spring onions. Remove lime leaves.

4 Cook prawn crackers in hot oil. Drain on absorbent paper. Fill crackers with about a heaped teaspoon of mixture and serve immediately.

M a k e s   3 0

C o o k ' s   T i p s

- *Laos, or galangal, is similar to ginger, which you can use as a substitute.*
- *Kaffir lime leaves are available dried. You can substitute crushed fresh lemon or lime leaves.*
- *Nam pla is a pungent fish sauce. If you do not have it, omit it.*
- *You can cook the crackers in advance and store them in an airtight container. Once filled, they'll go soggy, so fill them and serve as required.*

Sherry-coated Chicken Balls

Bamboo shoots and water chestnuts give these meatballs both flavour and texture. They can be made in advance and reheated in the microwave before serving. Serve them with toothpicks.

½ x 225-gram tin bamboo shoots, well drained
½ x 225-gram tin water chestnuts, well drained
50 grams mushrooms
2 cloves garlic, peeled
1 tblsp dark soy sauce

200 grams each of chicken and pork mince
2 tblsp chilli sauce
1 egg
2 tblsp chopped fresh coriander

Sauce

½ cup medium sherry
¼ cup brown sugar
1 tblsp minced ginger
pinch chilli powder

1 tblsp each plum and soy sauce
1 tsp cornflour

1 In a food processor, put the bamboo shoots, water chestnuts, mushrooms and garlic, and process until the mixture is finely chopped.

2 Add the mince meats, sauces, egg and coriander and pulse only until mixed.

3 Roll tablespoonfuls into balls. Deep-fry the balls at 180°C, or pan-fry in oil until the balls are golden and cooked. Drain on absorbent paper.

Sauce

1 In a large saucepan, put the sherry, brown sugar, ginger, plum and soy sauces, and chilli, and bring to the boil. Mix the cornflour with a little water to make a smooth paste. Pour into the sauce ingredients and stir over a moderate heat until thickened.

2 Toss the meatballs in the sauce. Transfer to a large serving dish and garnish with fresh coriander. Serve with toothpicks.

Cook's Tip

The meatballs can be reheated in the sauce. Do not boil too long as the sauce will break down.

Sweet Macadamia & Peanut Satay Sauce

Macadamia nuts make this satay a little different and the spices add gentle fragrant undertones.

1 tblsp minced chilli	1 tsp each ground cumin
2 tsp minced fresh root	and coriander
ginger	1/4 cup peanut oil
3 large juicy cloves garlic,	1 onion, peeled and finely
crushed, peeled and	chopped
chopped, or 2 tsp	250 grams roasted peanuts
minced	400-gram can coconut
70-gram packet	milk
macadamia nuts	2 tblsp brown sugar
3/4 tsp turmeric	1 tsp tamarind chutney
1/2 tsp white pepper	salt

1 In a food processor, or blender, process the chilli, ginger, garlic, macadamia nuts, turmeric, cumin, coriander and white pepper until a paste is formed.

2 Heat the oil in a saucepan or frying pan and cook the chilli mixture in oil over a moderate heat for 4-5 minutes, stirring regularly until very fragrant. Add the onion to the pan and continue to cook for a further 5 minutes until the onion has become soft.

3 Grind the nuts in a food processor until fine. Add to the sauce with the coconut milk, brown sugar, tamarind chutney and salt. Simmer 1-2 minutes.

4 Serve hot on kebabs of chicken, meat or fish.

Makes about 1 1/2 cups

Cook's Tip

A quick marinade for this satay: for 500 grams of diced meat or poultry, mix together 1 crushed clove garlic, about 3 tablespoons each of olive oil, soy sauce and sherry, and a good squeeze of lemon juice.

Wines for Eastern Flavours

The East has no tradition of wine drinking; food is usually consumed with green tea, beer or sake. This means that matching wine to the flavours of the East should be treated with some caution.

But, with a little experimentation, it is possible to achieve some great wine and food combinations with Eastern food.

Wines that have a touch of spice themselves are the best choice. Rieslings, both dry and medium, Gewurztraminers and oak-aged Sauvignon Blancs are good choices with Eastern food. Forget reds and stick with the whites, they work much better.

When matching wines with these flavours I usually avoid serving wine with dishes that have vinegar, as the flavour of the vinegar will make the wine taste sour. Also, watch for chilli. More than one chilli and you may not be able to taste the wine at all.

If the flavours are predominantly spicy, such as ginger, cinnamon or cumin, try a Gewurztraminer from Longridge of Hawkes Bay or Robard & Butler. And with strong fruit flavours such as mango or pineapple, match the food with a Riesling, such as Corbans Private Bin Amberley Rhine Riesling or Stoneleigh Vineyard Marlborough Rhine Riesling. For vegetable or herbal flavours, like coriander, look for a Sauvignon Blanc, and choose one that has a little oak if possible; look for Oak Aged or Fumé Blanc on the label, such as Longridge of Hawkes Bay Oak Aged Sauvignon Blanc or Corbans Private Bin Wood Aged Sauvignon Blanc.

Asian Chicken Liver Pâté

This chicken pâté is quick to prepare and, with a little bit of added spice, it's far better than the heavy gelatin glazed supermarket versions.

25 grams butter
1 small onion, peeled and
　finely chopped
2 tsp finely chopped fresh
　ginger
250 grams chicken livers

2 tsp ground cumin
2 tblsp dry sherry
2 tblsp cream
salt and pepper to taste
fresh coriander to garnish

1 Heat the butter in a frying pan and add the onion and ginger. Cook over a moderate heat until the onion has softened but is not coloured.

2 Trim the livers of the core and cut in half. Add the livers and cumin to the pan and toss over a moderate heat until the livers are almost cooked. Add the sherry and cream and bring to the boil for 1 minute.

3 Transfer the contents of the pan to a food processor and process until smooth. Season with salt and pepper to taste.

4 Transfer to a serving dish. Refrigerate, covered, until well chilled.

5 Serve garnished with coriander.

Makes about 1 1/2 cups

Crab & Ginger Wontons with Pawpaw Dip

Bite into these wontons for a real flavour burst from the sweet hot ginger.

170 grams white fish, such
　as gurnard or cod
2 spring onions, trimmed
　and roughly chopped
½ tsp sesame oil

2-cm piece stem ginger in
　syrup
200 grams fresh crabmeat
1 packet wonton wrappers
clean oil for deep-frying

1 Put the chopped white fish, spring onion and ginger in a food processor and process until well mixed and smooth. Pulse in the sesame oil and crabmeat.

2 Use the mixture to make wontons, following the instructions for folding on the back of the pack.

3 Deep-fry in hot oil for 4-5 minutes until golden. Drain well on absorbent paper.

4 Serve with Pawpaw Dip.

Makes about 50

Pawpaw Dip

½ pawpaw
1 tblsp lemon juice
1 tblsp chopped fresh
　coriander

1 tblsp finely chopped or
　minced shallots
2 tblsp orange juice

1 Peel pawpaw and remove seeds. Dice half the pawpaw very finely. Place remaining half in food processor and process until smooth.

2 Combine diced pawpaw, purée, lemon juice, coriander, shallots and orange juice.

Makes 3/4 cup

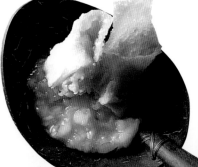

Thai Fresh Salmon Croquettes

These salmon cakes are quickly prepared using mini muffin tins. The sweet miso vinaigrette is a sharp contrast to the creamy rich salmon.

200 grams fresh salmon
    fillet
200 grams white fish, such
    as cod or snapper

1 egg
1 tsp Thai red curry paste
good dash salt

Topping

1 red chilli, de-seeded and minced
2 spring onions, trimmed and finely minced
2 tblsp finely chopped coriander

1 Remove the skin from salmon. Roughly chop salmon and white fish and process in a food processor with the egg, red curry paste and salt until the mixture is smooth.

2 Lightly oil 36 mini muffin tins. Place teaspoonfuls of mixture in each tin and press down with back of spoon. Brush tops lightly with oil.

3 Bake at 180°C for 10 minutes. Serve warm or cold with Sweet Miso Vinaigrette. Garnish with topping.

Makes 36

Topping

Mix together the chilli, spring onion and coriander.

Cook's Tip

If you do not have any mini muffin tins, these can be rolled into balls, dusted with flour and pan-fried in clarified butter.

Sweet Miso Vinaigrette

¾ cup boiling water
1 packet single serve miso soup
2 tblsp rice vinegar
½ tsp sugar

Pour boiling water over miso soup. Stir to dissolve. Cool a little and then add rice vinegar and sugar.

Cook's Tip

Thai curry paste is available in supermarkets. It keeps well in the refrigerator and is great to have on hand.

Sesame Beef Balls

Meatballs need not be dull and boring. These spicy morsels with a sweet glaze are a little different.

2 cloves garlic, peeled and
   mashed
2 spring onions, finely
   chopped
500 grams minced beef
1½ tsp five spice powder
salt and pepper
1 egg

2 tblsp dark soy sauce or
   Ketjap Manis
½ cup soft white
   breadcrumbs
2 tblsp cornflour
2 tblsp peanut oil
1 tsp sesame oil

Glaze

2 tblsp sesame seeds
2 tblsp soy sauce or Ketjap Manis
4 tblsp Hoisin sauce

1 Combine garlic, spring onions, beef, five spice powder, salt, pepper, soy sauce, egg and bread-crumbs. These may be mixed in a food processor, but be careful not to overprocess as it may end up more like sausage meat. Roll mixture into small walnut sized balls and toss in cornflour.

2 Heat oil and sesame oil in a large pan. Cook the meatballs, turning often until browned all over.

3 Add sesame seeds, soy sauce and Hoisin sauce to the pan. Shake the pan so meatballs are coated in glaze and sesame seeds brown.

4 Serve with toothpicks or skewers.

Makes 40-50

Variation

Roll the mixture around half a toasted walnut – yum.

Cook's Tip

Ketjap Manis is Indonesian soy sauce, and is sweeter and spicier than the usual Chinese soy sauce

Prawn & Vegetable Fritters with Cucumber Dipping Sauce

Baby seafood fritters with a difference – try them.

¾ cup rice flour

¾ cup self-raising flour

salt and pepper

2 eggs

¾ cup water

1 clove garlic, peeled and mashed

1 onion, peeled and grated

1 carrot, peeled and grated

1 tblsp finely chopped ginger

¼ cup diced green pepper

1 cup bean sprouts

300 grams peeled prawns or shrimps

clean oil for deep-frying

1 Place both flours, salt and pepper in bowl and make a well in the centre. Add eggs and water and beat until smooth. Add garlic, onion, carrot, ginger, green pepper, bean sprouts and prawns to the batter.

2 Place large teaspoonfuls (which include a prawn or shrimp) in hot oil. Cook until golden brown. Drain and serve with dipping sauce.

Makes about 30 fritters

Cucumber Dipping Sauce

2 cloves garlic, peeled and mashed

1 red chilli, de-seeded and diced

¼ cup white wine vinegar

¼ cup water

¼ cup finely diced or grated cucumber

¼ tsp salt

Combine garlic, chilli, vinegar, water, cucumber and salt.

Makes 1 cup

Cook's Tip

Deep-frying should be done at 180°C. It is best if you have a special electric deep fryer. At the very least, invest in a thermometer to keep track of the temperature. Deep-frying is definitely not recommended on an open gas flame.

Red Lentil & Onion Pakoras

This is a variation on Indian vegetable fritters made with chickpea flour batter. These are a little simpler, and nice with either of the following dipping sauces.

¼ cup red lentils

2 onions, peeled and grated

1 large carrot, peeled and grated

1 large potato, peeled and grated

1½ cups chickpea flour

1½ tsp baking powder

1 tsp each ground cumin, coriander and garam masala, ground black pepper and salt

¼ cup chopped fresh coriander

1 egg

¼ cup water

1 Soak the lentils in lots of cold water for 4 hours. Drain well through a sieve.

2 In a bowl, mix together the lentils, onion, carrot, potato, flour, spices, baking powder, coriander, egg and water to a stiff dough. Season well.

3 Heat oil to 180°C. Drop teaspoonfuls of the mixture into the hot oil, cooking about 8 at a time, until they are golden brown. They will float to the top when cooked and should be even in colour.

4 Remove from the hot oil with a slotted spoon and drain well on absorbent paper. Keep warm in a low oven while cooking the remainder.

5 Serve with one of the following dipping sauces.

Makes about 36

Cucumber & Mint Dipping Sauce

Peel and de-seed ½ telegraph cucumber. Grate the flesh and mix with 2 tblsp chopped mint and 1 cup non fat plain yoghurt.

Cheat's Mint Dipping Sauce

Slightly warm 1 cup bought Mint Jelly and mix with ¼ cup clear apple juice.

Scallops with Spices & Mango Sauce

The Kato spice rub that I have used here is flavoured with a blend of lime flesh, garlic, chillies and ginger. It goes well with the scallops, especially when accompanied with a puréed mango dipping sauce.

500 grams scallops
¼ cup Kato Wet Spice Rub
about 10 rashers streaky bacon

Mango Dipping Sauce

2 fresh mangoes
juice of 1 lime or lemon
1 shallot, finely minced

1 Wash and clean the scallops and pat dry on absorbent paper. Place the scallops into a bowl with the Wet Spice Rub and toss well. Cover and refrigerate for 30-60 minutes.

2 Trim the rind from the bacon and stretch the rashers using the back of a heavy cook's knife. This way you do not end up with heavy thick pieces of bacon around the delicate scallops.

3 Cut the rashers in half and wrap each half around two scallops on a bamboo skewer. Grill the scallops under a high heat for 4-5 minutes, turning to achieve an even colour. Serve them from a large dish with the Mango Sauce.

Makes about 36

Mango Sauce

Cut down the long side of the mango on each side of the stone. Peel and discard the stone and skin. Place the mango, lime juice and shallot into a food processor and process until smooth. If you do not have mango, use pawpaw. You will need about half a small pawpaw.

Cook's Tips

- *Remember, when cooking with bamboo skewers, to soak them in water for about 30 minutes at least. This way they will take longer to dry out under the grill and hopefully not burn. A second precaution is to place a piece of foil over the exposed parts of the bamboo stick when you are grilling.*

- *I do not buy bacon in plastic packs as I find it watery and tasteless. If available, buy bacon from the deli department at the supermarket. Streaky bacon is best for this recipe, as it has a little more fat in the rasher end and it stands up to the grilling better*

Bubbles, Oysters and More

When you have something very special to celebrate that calls for 'bubbles', take time to match the nibbles with the wine. Seafood and, in particular, oysters and salmon, makes a magical combination, reflected in the choice of recipes in this chapter.

Salmon Rillettes

This decadent recipe was demonstrated in Auckland by Anne Willan from La Varenne, France. The combination of smoked and fresh salmon is delightful.

125 grams soft unsalted
    butter
¼ clove garlic, peeled
100 grams smoked salmon
¼ cup white wine
    (preferably dry)
few parsley stalks
    (optional)
salt

200 grams salmon
    (2 medium size salmon
    steaks)
white pepper
grated nutmeg
1 tsp dry sherry (optional)
48 baby toasts
dill to garnish

1 Put 1 tblsp of the unsalted butter in a frying pan. Sauté garlic over a low heat for 3-4 minutes to cook but do not burn. Add smoked salmon and cook only until salmon has changed colour to a soft pink. Transfer to a plate.

2 Heat a second tblsp of unsalted butter in a small saucepan with wine and parsley stalks. Add salmon steaks, cover and poach over a low heat for 4-5 minutes until steaks are just cooked. Remove from the liquid. Cool.

3 Using forks, carefully tear the smoked salmon into small pieces. Do the same to the steaks, discarding skin and bone.

4 In a bowl, beat remaining butter until creamy. With a fork, carefully add both salmon mixtures, making sure you don't turn the mixture into pate – it should be coarse. Season with salt, white pepper and nutmeg. If you wish, add a teaspoon of dry sherry.

5 Serve on baby toasts garnished with dill.

Makes 48

Catherine's Seafood Fritters with Lime & Dill Mayonnaise

This recipe was designed by colleague and friend Catherine Bell for The Good Taste Company using their products.

¾ cup flour

1 tsp baking powder

good dash salt and pepper

½ tsp curry powder

1 clove garlic, peeled and
    mashed

2 tblsp chopped parsley,
    preferably Italian

1 tblsp chopped fresh dill

1 red chilli, de-seeded and
    finely chopped

1 tblsp chilli sauce

¼ cup milk

3 eggs, separated

500 grams mixed seafood,
    diced (scallops,
    prawns, fish, whitebait)

clarified butter

1 packet The Good Taste
    Company Lime and
    Dill mayonnaise

1 Sift the flour, baking powder, salt, pepper and curry powder into a bowl. Stir in the garlic, parsley, dill and chilli.

2 In another bowl mix together the chilli sauce, milk and egg yolks. Pour into the dry ingredients and blend together. Fold in the seafood.

3 In a clean bowl, beat the egg whites until stiff but not dry. Fold into the batter.

4 Heat a good knob of clarified butter in a frying pan and cook tablespoonfuls of the batter mix. Allow about 2 minutes on each side. The fritters should be ever so slightly undercooked so that they are moist and not dry.

5 Keep warm in a 150°C oven while cooking the rest of the batter mix. Serve with the mayonnaise as a dip for the fritters.

Makes about 24

Scallop Tartlets with Garlic & Pinenut Crunch

These are particularly garlicky and very more-ish. Quickly sautéed and topped with a crumble in a buttery pastry case, these scallops are great any time.

400 grams short pastry,
  bought or pre-made
  (recipe follows)
500 grams scallops
50 grams clarified butter
¼ cup pinenuts, chopped
¼ cup fresh white
  breadcrumbs
grated rind 2 lemons

¼ cup chopped Italian
  parsley
2 cloves garlic, crushed
  and mashed to a paste
2 shallots or spring onions,
  finely chopped
2 tblsp double cream
  (optional)
salt and pepper

1 Roll out the pastry and use it to line 36 baby tartlet tins. Bake blind at 200°C for 15 minutes, or until the pastry is cooked. Cool and store in an airtight container.

2 Wash and trim the scallops. Pat dry on an absorbent paper towel.

3 Heat half the butter in a frying pan and add the pinenuts and breadcrumbs and toss until both are lightly golden. Remove from the heat and stir in the parsley and the grated lemon rind.

4 Heat the remaining butter in a large frying pan until quite hot. Toss in the garlic, shallots and scallops, and toss until the scallops are just cooked. *If you are in any doubt over this, take one out and try it (cook's perk!), because there is nothing worse than overcooked scallops.*

5 Add the cream and toss well. Season with salt and pepper. Place a scallop into each warmed tartlet case, sprinkle over a little of the pinenut topping and serve.

Makes approx 3 dozen

Basic Short Pastry

2 cups flour
1 tsp salt

150 grams butter
4-5 tblsp water

Sift the flour and salt into a bowl. Cut in the butter until the mixture resembles fine crumbs. Stir in sufficient water with a knife until the dough comes together. Turn out onto a floured surface and bring together. Knead lightly. Rest 10 minutes.

Potato Blini with Toppings

Making potato blinis cuts down the time it takes to make yeast blinis, but they need to be eaten while fresh and warm.

450 grams potatoes, peeled and quartered
3 eggs
¼ cup self-raising flour
2 tblsp melted butter
½ cup each hot milk and hot cream
salt
clarified butter for pan-frying

1 Cook the potatoes in boiling salted water until tender. Drain well and return to a clean saucepan over a moderate heat, shaking the pan until the potatoes are steamed dry.

2 Sieve the potatoes to make a smooth lump-free mash. Cool for 30 minutes before beating in the eggs, flour, butter, hot milk and cream. Season well with salt.

3 Heat a good knob of butter in a frying pan and cook tablespoonfuls of the mixture to make baby pikelet size cakes. Cook until bubbles appear on the surface. Flip and cook the other side. Keep warm in a 150°C oven until all the mixture has been cooked.

4 Top with one of the following ideas and serve slightly warm.

Makes about 30

Toppings

- Smoked salmon with crème fraîche or sour cream, caviar and dill.

- Sour cream, caviar and chives.

- Smoked eel, with crumbled pan-fried bacon and a dollop of sour cream.

- Salmon Rillettes (see page 44).

47

Oysters

Oysters are one of those foods that people's eyes light up at the mere thought of. I have never really become a lover of oysters, however, so Warwick ends up with my share as well! Served in the half shell on a bed of crushed ice or rock salt, or out of the shell in a dish with dipping sauces, oysters are one of the loveliest foods to match with Champagne.

Shell or Not?

Ask your fishmonger to get you oysters in the half shell. Keep them in the coldest part of the refrigerator until ready to serve. Freshly shucked oysters should be kept in one layer, shell-side down, covered with a damp tea towel. They will last for 2 days, but your fridge must be very cold.

Do not wash them, but pick out any shell that may be left on them. Loosen the oyster from the shell carefully with a sharp knife for your guests. Provide a jar of toothpicks or baby forks for guests to serve themselves.

Bluff oysters are usually only available shelled. Serve these well chilled in a bowl sitting in a bed of ice with dipping sauce. These are usually expensive and therefore I maintain they are nicest served naturally, with buttered bread that has character, not flabby white packet bread, and with lemon wedges on the side.

The 'R' Rule

The rule about not eating oysters during the months which have an 'r' in their name has two origins. One is that these are the warmer months, and before refrigeration oysters did not keep well; also during summer they spawn, leaving them soft and fatty.

Oyster Overload

With the ideas that follow I have only spooned a little dressing over each oyster so as not to detract from the oyster's delicate taste.

Naturally

Place the oyster well chilled on a bed of rock salt or crushed ice. Serve accompanied with buttered bread and lemon wedges.

With Caviar

Top each oyster in the half shell with a small dollop of crème fraîche or sour cream. Spoon over a little caviar and garnish with grated lemon rind and chopped parsley. Serve with buttered brown bread. Again choose a good bread, such as a brown sourdough.

'Nu Awlins' Style

Sprinkle a drop or two of Tabasco sauce over each oyster and decorate with chives.

Champagne Sabayon

Peel and finely dice 4 shallots and place in a saucepan with 1 cup of Champagne. Boil until 2 tablespoons remain. Remove the saucepan from the heat and quickly whisk in 175 grams softened butter. Do not allow the butter to melt; it has to emulsify. When all the butter is added, set aside. In the top of a double saucepan whisk 3 tblsp Champagne with 2 egg yolks until thick and foamy. Fold this foam into the butter sauce. Spoon a little over each oyster and then place on a bed of salt. Grill under a high heat until the Sabayon has slightly browned and puffed. Serve immediately with baby forks. Enough for 24 oysters.

Dressed From The Orient

Mince or finely chop 2 spring onions. Use as much green as there is white. Mix with ½ cup rice wine vinegar, grated rind 1 lemon and 1 tsp finely minced fresh ginger. Spoon a smidgen over each oyster before serving. Or, if the oysters are out of the shell, serve the dressing in a small dish for dipping. Enough for 24 oysters.

Coriander & Orange

Mix together the juice of 1 orange, lemon and lime. De-seed and mince 1 very small red pepper and stir into the juice with 1 tsp minced fresh ginger and a dash of sesame oil. Just before spooning a little over each oyster, stir in about ½ tblsp chopped fresh coriander. Serve over the oysters or in a small bowl for dipping. Enough for 24 oysters.

In A Roasted Red Pepper Dressing

Grill 1 red pepper until black. Cool, peel, discard seeds, core and place the pepper in a food processor. Blend in ½ clove garlic, peeled, ½ tsp minced ginger, 1 tblsp minced onion, few leaves fresh Italian parsley, ¼ cup olive oil and 2 tblsp white wine vinegar. Process until smooth. Pour a spoonful over each oyster and garnish with baby lettuce leaves or parsley leaves. Enough for 24 oysters.

Heavenly

Remember 'Angels On Horseback' – oysters wrapped in bacon – well, people loved them, so try this. Grill 3 rashers bacon until crispy, then crumble. Mince or finely chop 6 prunes and blend with bacon and ½ cup of double cream in a saucepan. Pour over the oysters and warm under a grill for a minute. Sprinkle with chopped parsley and serve slightly warm.

Mexican

Top each oyster with a spoonful of guacamole and serve garnished with fresh chopped coriander.

Bacon & Balsamic

Heat 1 tblsp butter in a frying pan. Add 4 peeled and chopped shallots, 1 peeled and mashed clove garlic and 3 trimmed rashers bacon finely diced. Cook until fragrant. Pour in ½ cup Champagne and bring to the boil. Allow to boil until reduced by half and then add 1 teaspoon balsamic vinegar. Spoon over the oysters and warm under a grill.

Other Ways with Oysters

Be careful when cooking oysters, as they overcook quickly. All they really need is to be just heated.

Buttery Filo Rolls

30 oysters
¾ cup crème fraîche
2 tblsp minced chives
about 15 sheets filo pastry
100-125 grams butter, melted

1 Loosen the oysters from the shell and set aside. Blend the crème fraîche and the chives together.

2 Cut filo pastry sheets into half lengthwise. Brush each filo sheet with butter and fold in half crosswise. Spread the filo with a thin layer of crème fraîche and place an oyster on top. Bring the sides over and then roll up to enclose the oyster and place on a greased baking tray. Repeat using all the oysters and crème fraîche. Brush the tops with remaining melted butter.

3 Bake at 200°C for 10 minutes or until golden. Serve warm.

Makes 30

Oysters In Beer Batter

The beer makes an easy light batter, and once cooked the beer can't be tasted.

1 cup flour	36 oysters
1 egg, separated	1 tblsp chopped dill
1 egg yolk	about ½ cup seasoned
50 grams butter, melted	flour
1 cup beer	oil for deep frying

1 Sift the flour into a bowl and make a well in the centre. Beat the egg yolks together and stir into the well with the melted butter and the beer. Cover and set aside for 1 hour.

2 Whisk the egg white in a clean bowl until it forms stiff peaks. Fold into the batter.

3 Toss the oysters in dill and seasoned flour. Shake off the excess so that hardly any remains. Dip into the batter and then deep-fry at 180°C until the fritters are golden and risen to the top.

4 Drain on absorbent paper and serve immediately.

5 Serve hot, if wished with Chilli and Chive Sauce or alternatively fresh lemon juice.

Makes 36

Chilli & Chive Sauce

To the basic mayonnaise recipe (page 69) add 1 tblsp chilli sauce, ½ tsp Worcestershire sauce, 1 tomato (peeled de-seeded and diced finely) and 1 tblsp each finely chopped chives and Italian parsley.

Sparkling Wines

Sparkling wine, Méthode Champenoise, Champagne – whatever you call it, wine with bubbles is special. It's one of the few wines that is just as enjoyable at breakfast as it is at a midnight celebration.

Most bottle-fermented bubblies available in New Zealand are known as Méthode Champenoise, but as from late 1995 you will see them labelled as Méthode Traditionelle.

The term Champagne is now only used for wines made in the Champagne region of France. The French Champagne producers also felt that the term Méthode Champenoise was too similar to Champagne, so that too has been banned.

Sparkling wines come in a wide range of styles and sweetness levels, so it should be simple to select one to suit your taste. Wine labelled Extra Brut is totally dry; Brut is dry; Sec is medium dry; Demi-sec is medium. There are also the Asti-style wines, which are sweet.

Many sparkling wines don't show a vintage date as they are a blend of more than one vintage. These wines are known as NV or non-vintage. Rosé or pink sparkling wines are sometimes made by adding a little red wine to the white.

Always serve sparkling wine in tall tulip-shaped glasses. The shape helps to retain the bubbles; the wine will quickly go flat in wide saucer-shaped glasses.

I find you get much better bubbles if the glasses are always hand-washed and rinsed. Never put good wine glasses in a dishwasher, it will taint the wine and kill the bubbles.

When matching food with sparkling wines, stick to mostly light, delicate flavours. Seafood, eggs, creamy dishes, mild lemon, salty and smokey foods all work well with bubblies such as Amadeus Méthode Champenoise, Champernay or Diva Marlborough Cuvée. For dishes with a bit more bite, try a Rosé style or fruity sparkling wine, such as Italiano Spumante or Diva Marlborough Cuvée, as they are most adaptable to going well with lightly spiced dishes, including dishes with garlic and even chilli.

Crab Cakes with Spicy Mayonnaise Dip

These are even more delicious if you have fresh crabmeat. Serve them hot.

25 grams butter
2 tblsp flour
¾ cup milk
310-gram can crabmeat, well drained
1½ tsp horseradish sauce
1 tsp dry mustard
2½ cups fresh white breadcrumbs
2 tblsp each cream and olive oil
2 eggs, separated
oil for deep-frying

1 Heat the butter in a saucepan and stir in the flour. Stir over a moderate heat for about 2 minutes until it is frothy. Gradually stir in the milk and cook over a moderate heat until the sauce has thickened.

2 Stir in the crabmeat, horseradish and mustard and remove from the heat.

3 Put the breadcrumbs in a bowl and pour in the cream and olive oil. Allow to stand for 1 minute. Blend the breadcrumbs and egg yolks into the saucepan.

4 Beat the egg whites in a clean bowl until they are stiff but not dry. Fold the egg whites gently into the crab mixture.

5 Heat the oil to 180°C. Deep-fry spoonfuls of the mixture until they are golden and have risen to the top. Drain well on absorbent paper and keep warm in a 140°C oven until the remaining mixture has been cooked.

6 Serve with Tabasco Mayonnaise Dipping Sauce.

Makes 30

Tabasco Mayonnaise Dipping Sauce

2 tomatoes, blanched and peeled
1 cup mayonnaise (preferably homemade, see page 69)
1 tblsp mustard (Dijon or wholeseed is nice)
1 tsp each horseradish and Tabasco sauce
2 tblsp each chopped chives and parsley
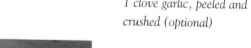
1 clove garlic, peeled and crushed (optional)

1 Cut the tomatoes in half horizontally and squeeze out the seeds and pulp from inside. Cut the remaining flesh into very small dice.

2 In a bowl, blend together all the ingredients. Season with salt and pepper if wished.

3 Keep refrigerated in an airtight container and serve well chilled.

Makes 1 ½ cups

Quails' Eggs, Radishes & Salt

The freshest ingredients presented well make the loveliest nibbles. I adore radishes and eggs with plenty of salt. Place well-washed radishes and peeled hardboiled quails' eggs on a plate. Add a pot of sea salt and a pot of homemade mayonnaise. Guests can then dip and dunk.

Cook's Tip

Quails' eggs are dainty little beige-shelled eggs and their size allows for a delightful presentation. To hard boil them, carefully place them in a pot of boiling water and stir for the first minute (this will help centre the egg yolk). Continue to gently boil for a further 3 minutes before plunging them into cold water to stop them over-cooking. Crack the shells gently and while still warm.

Smoked Calamari in Filo Cases

A buttery tender filo case filled with smoked calamari is a perfect partner for a glass of bubbles.

8 sheets filo pastry
100 grams butter, melted

Filling

3 rashers bacon, trimmed of rind
1 tblsp oil
2 tblsp minced shallots
100-gram packet smoked calamari
2 tblsp crème fraîche
snipped chives or spring onions to garnish

1 Cut each filo pastry sheet into 15 equal squares. Brush 3 squares with butter and place them into a mini muffin tin, each time twisting the next square a little so that you have uneven edges. Repeat with remaining filo – you will have enough for 36 mini muffin tins.

2 Bake at 200°C for about 7-10 minutes until the filo is lightly golden. Keep the cases in an airtight container. When ready to use, fill with a table-spoon of filling and garnish with snipped chives or spring onion.

Makes 36

Filling

Finely shred the bacon. Heat the oil in a frying pan and cook the bacon until crisp and brown. In a bowl, mix together the bacon, shallots, calamari and crème fraîche, and season with a little pepper if wished

Mainly Mediterranean

If you are like me and love foods like olives, sun-dried tomatoes and red peppers, capers and Parmesan, then this chapter is full of ideas especially for you.

Baby Smoked Pork Calzone

Pizza dough cut into baby rounds and stuffed with pinenuts, smoked pork and garlic, served hot from the oven.

1 basic pizza dough
   recipe (see page 57)
2 tblsp olive oil
½ onion, peeled and
   diced
2 cloves garlic, peeled
   and diced
¼ cup pinenuts
100 grams smoked
   pork, shredded
1 sun-dried red pepper
   in oil, drained and
   sliced
¼ cup chopped fresh
   herbs (oregano,
   basil, parsley,
   rosemary)
2 tblsp chopped capers
½ cup grated
   mozzarella cheese
pepper to season with
about 2 tblsp olive oil
   for glazing

1 Have the pizza dough made and proving while preparing the filling.

2 Put the oil in a frying pan and add the onion, garlic and pinenuts and cook 1-2 minutes. Remove from heat and cool. Stir in the pork, red pepper, herbs, capers and cheese. Remove from the heat and season well with pepper.

3 Roll the dough out to ½ cm thickness and cut into 5-cm rounds. Brush the edges with a little water and place a teaspoon of the mix in the middle. Fold in half to make a semi-circle. Place on a greased baking tray or hot pizza stone. Brush with oil to glaze.

4 Fan bake at 220°C for 5-8 minutes until hot and golden. Serve warm in a basket.

Makes about 30

Olive Dippers with Roasted Tomato Sauce

I have added black olives to a pizza dough, then cut the dough into small pieces, deep-fried it and served it hot with a light tomato sauce made from roasted summer tomatoes. These can be made in advance and re-heated in the oven before serving.

1 basic pizza dough recipe (see page 57)
½ cup stoned black olives
vegetable oil for deep frying

Roasted Tomato Sauce

2 large juicy summer tomatoes
handful of fresh Italian parsley
salt and pepper
½-1 tsp balsamic vinegar (or use cider vinegar)

1 Prepare the pizza dough to step 1 in the basic recipe. Add the olives to the flour and process with the remaining ingredients. Continue following the basic method (the dough will be black with olives). Allow to prove as instructed.

2 Roll the dough out to a 2 cm depth. Then, using a floured knife or round cutter, cut the dough into 2-cm rounds or square pieces.

3 Heat the oil to 180°C and deep-fry the pieces of dough until they are golden. *The olive doughs will be cooked once the olives have risen to the top. Make sure that they are nicely brown.* Drain on absorbent paper and keep warm. Serve with the Roasted Tomato Sauce.

Serves about 6-8

Roasted Tomato Sauce

Cut the large juicy tomatoes in half and place on a foil-lined baking tray. Bake at 240°C for about 15 minutes, until they have softened and the skins have blackened. Remove from the oven to cool. Discard the charred skins and process with the parsley, salt, pepper and vinegar until smooth.

Pizza Dough

This dough is easy to make and use. You can make baby pizza, by cutting the dough into small rounds, or baby garlic and pizza breads. This yeast dough is the basis for many fabulous nibbles that are both delicious and filling.

½ cup warm water
1 tsp yeast
½ tsp sugar
250 grams flour
½ tsp salt
about 2 tblsp olive oil

1 Mix the water, yeast and sugar together in a jug and set aside for 10 minutes until frothy.

2 Put the flour and salt into a food processor and, with the motor running, pour in the olive oil and yeast mixture and process to form a smooth dough. (Add a little more flour or oil if needed.)

3 Transfer to a lightly oiled bowl, cover with plastic wrap and set aside for about 1 hour, or until it is double in bulk.

4 Roll out the dough, cut into 5-cm rounds and

place on a hot oven tray. Top quickly with your favourite pizza topping and fan bake at 240°C for 5-8 minutes, until crispy and golden.

M a k e s   a b o u t   3 0

Topping Ideas

- Bocconcini and lemon-infused olive oil.

- Sliced cherry tomatoes, Parmesan and oregano.

- Tapenade and cheese.

- Roasted garlic and mozzarella.

- Salami and red pepper pate.

- Olive oil, grated Parmesan and black pepper.

- Raw prawns and pesto.

- Roasted aubergines and sliced tomatoes

Grilled Focaccia with Tomato & Mushroom Paste

Focaccia (well-flavoured, chewy Italian bread) is ideal as the basis for a substantial nibble. Beware of thin bread sold with salty, over-herbed toppings masquerading as focaccia.

1 large red pepper
25 grams butter or 2 tblsp oil from the tomatoes
1 clove garlic, peeled and mashed
100 grams mushrooms, very finely sliced
2 tsp chopped fresh oregano
200 gram bottle sun-dried tomatoes in olive oil, well drained
pepper
4-6 basil leaves
one round of focaccia bread (see page 59)
¼ cup freshly grated Parmesan cheese

1 Grill the red pepper under a very high heat until well blackened. Place in a plastic bag and leave until cool. When cool enough to handle, peel the skin away and remove the core and seeds. *This is easiest done under cold running water.*

2 Heat butter or oil in a frying pan and cook garlic and mushrooms for 5-7 minutes or until mushrooms are soft.

3 Put red pepper and tomatoes in a food processor, and purée until well blended. Add some of the reserved oil if necessary to make a thick purée. Stir purée into mushroom mixture. Season with pepper and roughly pinched basil leaves and oregano. Spread tomato and mushroom mixture on top of focaccia and sprinkle with Parmesan cheese.

Focaccia Bread

¼ cup warm water
1 tsp sugar
2½ tsp dry yeast or 18 grams fresh yeast
2 cups water at room temperature
¼ cup good olive oil
1 kg flour
olive oil to brush with
1 tblsp fine sea salt

1 Mix ¼ cup water and sugar together in a small bowl. Sprinkle yeast over, stir well and set aside in a warm place for 10 minutes or until frothy.

2 Stir frothed mixture into the 2 cups of warm water and olive oil.

3 Put flour into a food processor and pulse to sift. With the machine running, pour liquid and oil down feed tube as fast as the flour can absorb it. After the dough gathers into a mass, process it for a further 20 seconds. Turn onto a floured board and knead for 2-3 minutes.

4 Place dough in a lightly oiled bowl and cover with oiled plastic wrap. Set aside for 1-1½ hours or until doubled in bulk.

5 Divide dough into 2 or 3 portions and roll out each to a 25-30 cm round and place on a greased baking tray. Cover with a tea-towel and set aside in a warm place for 30 minutes. Dimple dough with your fingers. Cover again with tea-towel and leave in a warm place for 30 minutes to 1 hour or until doubled in bulk.

6 Liberally brush with olive oil and sprinkle sea salt and/or herbs over the top. Bake at 200°C for 20-25 minutes, spraying with water 3 times during first 10 minutes.

Makes 3 loaves

Cook's Tip

Unless you have a very cold kitchen, there's no need to put the bowl in a hot water cupboard. Wrap the bowl in a towel and set aside out of any draught.

4 Place under a moderately hot grill until cheese has softened and topping is hot. Cut into wedges to serve.

Serves 6-8

Cook's Tips

- *To crush garlic easily, press down on the clove with a large knife. The skin will break away from the clove at the stem end and you can peel it quickly and easily.*
- *If you only have plain sun-dried tomatoes, add 2-3 tblsps of olive oil to them when puréeing.*
- *Use freezer bags for cooling peppers as they will withstand the heat of the grilled pepper.*

Antipasto Platter

I prepare my antipasto platters with foods that I like. I'm not sure whether they are made up of all the correct foods, but I don't really mind, so long as the food is enjoyed. This is just a list of the items that I most often enjoy. It really is a platter full of good flavours, tastes and textures; and it is so easy for people to help themselves.

- Roasted and marinated slices of peppers of all colours – I marinate them up in a good vinaigrette flavoured heavily with seasonal herbs.

- Bowls of olives, marinated and plain.

- Tapenades for spreading, such as sun-dried red pepper or tomato (see page 67), and olive (see page 69).

- Well-drained and flaked pieces of canned tuna.

- Cherry tomatoes, or slices of really ripe tasty summer tomatoes.

- Quartered and grilled fennel bulbs – scrumptious if you can obtain baby ones. Brush with olive oil and grill or pan-fry.

- Slices of meat – salami, rare roast beef or ham.

- Cheeses, such as bocconcini and feta (plain or marinated).

- Breads, such as olive, sliced French, pita or hot pizza dough.

- Mussels or clams that have been cooked and marinated in a little tomato vinaigrette or

with plenty of herbs.

- Marinated artichokes, deep-fried caper berries or capers.

- Bowls of homemade mayonnaise to dip into, perhaps flavoured with olives

Matching with Mediterranean

The flavours of the Mediterranean love wine, especially red wine. Nowhere in this region is food consumed without a glass of the local product to complement and enhance the occasion.

The sort of wines I prefer to serve with Mediterranean foods are not heavy, or too oaky. Wines that are fruity and soft on the finish are best; Pinot Noir, Merlot and a lighter style Cabernet/Merlot are my choices. Try and find wines that are not too young, they will be softer and not so acidic.

If you prefer a white wine that will match these foods, try an oak-aged Sauvignon Blanc. The light touch of oak will soften the herbaceousness in the wine and provide a better match than straight Sauvignon Blanc.

Two of my favourite wine matches for Mediterranean foods are oak-aged Sauvignon Blancs, such as Longridge of Hawkes Bay or Corbans Private Bin, with pesto, tomato and red peppers, and Merlot or Pinot Noir, such as Cottage Block Pinot Noir or Longridge of Hawkes Bay Cabernet Sauvignon Merlot, with eggplant, olives and garlic.

Remember when selecting a wine, match strongly flavoured foods with rich, robust wines. Delicate flavours need a light wine style that doesn't overpower the food.

Green Olive Paste

This green olive version of tapenade makes a wonderful topping for crostini, especially when garnished with slices of grilled red peppers and toasted almond flakes.

375-gram jar large green olives (I used Spanish ones)
1-2 tsp capers
4 anchovies, well drained of oil
1 clove garlic, peeled
¼ cup good olive oil
good sprinkling of ground cumin
1 tblsp ground almonds

1 Stone the green olives and place into a food processor with all the remaining ingredients. Process until the mixture forms a smooth paste.

2 Store in an airtight container in the refrigerator.

Makes about 1 cup

Cannelini Bean & Garlic Spread

A heady purée of garlic and beans to put on crackers and crusty bread. Marvellously healthy too.

2 small potatoes, peeled
2-3 tblsp olive oil
4 cloves garlic, peeled and chopped
1 large onion, peeled and diced
2 tblsp sour cream

310-gram can cannelini beans (well drained)
about 2 tblsp chopped fresh parsley and oregano
white pepper and salt to season

1 Cook the potatoes in boiling salted water until they are tender. Drain well and place in a processor.

2 Heat the olive oil in a frying pan and add the garlic and onions. Cook over a low heat for about 15 minutes, until the onions and garlic are soft and translucent. *Do not have the heat too high, as you will burn the garlic before it is cooked.*

3 Put the onions into the food processor with the potatoes, beans and sour cream, and process until the mixture is smooth and creamy. Pulse in the herbs and then season well with the white pepper and salt.

4 Chill and then serve.

Makes about 1 1/2 cups

Variation

Use a can of well-drained chickpeas in place of the cannelini beans, and add 2 tblsp finely chopped fennel in place of the oregano and parsley.

George's Tomato Flan

Rich in tomato taste, I enjoy this flan at home with a favourite Uncle George who, at 83, still cooks every day. After spending almost 10 years in Spain, he has a penchant for olives, tomatoes and anchovies. This can be cut into hearty-size wedges or smaller slices; it's up to you.

1 medium sized onion, peeled and chopped	4 eggs
50 grams butter	1 cup grated tasty cheddar cheese
dash olive oil	400-gram packet short pastry
2 cloves garlic, peeled and crushed	50-gram can of anchovies, drained and rinsed
2 x 400-gram cans chopped tomatoes	black olives, about 12
2 tblsp chopped fresh basil	basil leaves to garnish
salt and pepper	

1 Cook onion in butter and oil until golden, add garlic and tomatoes. Simmer for about 45 minutes, stirring regularly, until mixture is thick. When cool, beat in eggs, cheese and basil. Season to taste.

2 Roll out pastry on a floured board and use to line the base and sides of a 24-cm loose-bottom flan tin. Prick with a fork and bake blind for 8-10 minutes at 190°C.

3 Fill pastry case with mixture and top with the anchovies and olives. Return to a 180°C oven and bake for 20-30 minutes. Garnish when cool with basil.

4 Serve in wedges, or alternatively bake as individual tartlets.

Makes 12-16 wedges

Chicken Almond Filo Surprises

Chicken flavoured with spices, nuts and herbs wrapped in buttery light layers of filo pastry and served warm – just delicious.

1 large double breast of
chicken, skin removed
¼ cup white wine
1 tblsp butter
1 small onion, peeled and
diced
1 clove garlic, peeled and
mashed
1 tblsp flour
½ tsp ground cinnamon

1 tsp each ground
coriander and ginger
¾ cup chicken stock
1 tblsp lemon juice
salt and pepper
¼ cup sliced almonds
¼ cup chopped parsley
about 20 sheets filo pastry
¼ cup melted butter
flaked almonds to garnish

1 Place chicken in frying pan and pour over the wine. Bring to the boil, lower heat and simmer for 20 minutes. Reserve the liquid.

2 Heat butter in a saucepan and cook onion and garlic for 2 minutes. Add flour, coriander, ginger and cinnamon, and cook a further minute. Add chicken stock and wine that chicken was cooked in. Bring to the boil and simmer 1-2 minutes. Set aside.

3 Shred chicken into small strips. Add chicken, lemon juice, salt, pepper, almonds and parsley to sauce.

4 Brush 1 sheet of pastry with butter and fold lengthwise into thirds. Place a spoonful of chicken mixture at end of each. Fold ends over to form triangles and continue folding in triangle pattern to end of pastry.

5 Place on a greased baking tray and brush with butter and decorate with a few flaked almonds. Repeat until all the pastry and filling is used.

6 Bake at 190°C for 15-20 minutes or until golden brown.

Makes 20

Cherry Tomatoes &
Ricotta Tartlets

These cheesy tartlets are ideal warm or cold.

2 eggs
¾ cup ricotta cheese
½ cup cream
½ tsp each salt and pepper
2 tblsp chopped fresh basil and oregano
4 sheets Ernest Adams Savoury Pastry Sheets
1 punnet cherry tomatoes, halved
¼ cup grated fresh Parmesan cheese

1 Lightly beat eggs together. Sieve the ricotta cheese and blend into the egg with the cream, salt, pepper, basil and oregano.

2 Cut pastry into 8-cm circles and use to line the base and sides of 40 patty tins. Re-roll of pastry also to line tins.

3 Half fill each tartlet with ricotta mixture and place a couple of tomato halves on top. Sprinkle with a little Parmesan cheese.

4 Bake at 180°C for 20-25 minutes or until golden and the filling is set.

M a k e s   a b o u t   4 0

Crostini

Bread toasts topped with all manner of good things are some of the easiest and most delightful ways to enjoy nibbles. Crostini can be topped with almost anything, all you need is a little imagination. These are my ideas, which are based around recipes in the book or foods that you can easily make or buy.

- Green Olive Paste (page 62) with toasted flaked almonds and finely diced red peppers.

- Tapenade (page 69) with blue cheese grilled or crumbled on top.

- Walnut Paste (page 67) with smoked pork and Italian parsley.

- Basil Pesto topped with bocconcini and fine shreds of sun-dried red peppers.

- Roasted and finely shredded peppers with double or triple cream Brie.

- Artichoke paste or sliced marinated artichokes with Cucumber & Chive Mayonnaise (page 69).

- Salmon or Smoked Chicken Rillettes (pages 44 and 82).

- Peeled, de-seeded and diced tomatoes tossed in a vinaigrette heavily scented with fresh basil.

- Roasted Eggplant with Garlic (see page 68), with maybe black olives and oregano to garnish.

- Parsley Pesto with Parmesan shavings (page 69).

To Make Crostini

I buy a fresh French loaf and cut it into slices about ½-1 cm wide. Brush liberally with olive oil, to which a smidgen of mashed garlic has been added, and then bake them at 200°C until they have become a little crisper. I do not cook them until they dry out completely, as when guests bite into them they will crumble.

Sun-dried Tomato or Red Pepper Paste

This paste is delicious made with either tomatoes or peppers. As the flavour is quite intense, I add a roasted tomato to soften the flavour and extend the expensive ingredients.

150 grams sun-dried tomatoes or
*   red peppers in oil*
2 cloves garlic, peeled
few sprigs fresh parsley,
*   preferably Italian*
1 small tomato (or ½ medium),
*   roasted*
few shakes Tabasco sauce
1-2 tblsp grated fresh Parmesan cheese
freshly ground black pepper and salt

1 Drain the tomatoes well of their oil, but keep the oil. Put the tomatoes, garlic, parsley, tomato and Tabasco Sauce in a food processor or small blender and process until the mixture is smooth. Add the reserved oil or fresh olive oil to reach a smooth paste. You may need an extra 1-2 tblsp depending on how well drained the tomatoes were.

2 Add the Parmesan cheese to taste. If you like the paste stronger in flavour, then add all the Parmesan. Season if wished with pepper and a little salt.

M a k e s   a b o u t   3/4   c u p

C o o k ' s   T i p s

- *Kept in the refrigerator, it will last for about 2 weeks, unless you are like us and eat it all in one sitting!*
- *To roast a tomato, place it on a piece of foil on an oven tray and bake at 220°C for 12-15 minutes until it is well browned and cooked.*

Walnut Paste

Slightly roasted walnuts add a deeper flavour.

150 grams walnuts,
*   roasted*
¼ cup grated Parmesan
*   cheese*
1 small clove of garlic,
*   peeled or crushed*
juice of half a lemon
½ tsp paprika

grated rind from half a
*   lemon*
¼ tsp ground nutmeg
½ tsp freshly ground white
*   pepper*
1 tsp salt
about ¼ cup olive oil

1 Put the walnuts, Parmesan, garlic, lemon juice, lemon rind, paprika, nutmeg, white pepper and salt into a food processor fitted with a chopping blade and process until all ingredients are finely chopped.

2 With the motor running gradually pour the olive oil down the feed tube until all of the oil has been incorporated and you have a smooth paste of spreading consistency. Store the walnut paste in clean sterile jars in the refrigerator.

M a k e s   1 ¹/2   c u p s

Clockwise from bottom left:
Sun-dried Tomato Paste &
Blue Cheese, Pesto,
Boconccini & sliced
Sun-dried Red
Peppers, Walnut
Paste with Smoked
Pork & Herbs.
Centre:
Artichokes with
Cucumber
Mayonnaise,
topped with
lemon rind.

Roasted
Eggplant with Garlic

**So simple to prepare, this can be served on top
of crostini or puréed and folded into some
lightly whipped cream and served as a pâté or
dip. It is great either way.**

*1 medium eggplant
salt
2-3 tblsp virgin olive oil
2 tblsp fresh lemon juice or
red wine vinegar*

*3 cloves garlic, peeled and
crushed
few leaves of oregano
½ tsp cracked black pepper
herbs to garnish*

1 Make sure that the
eggplant is firm and has no
blemishes at all. Cut into
1-cm wide slices and place in a
colander. Sprinkle with a light dusting
of salt and allow to stand for about 10 minutes
until the eggplant begins to weep. Pat the slices
dry with an absorbent paper towel.

2 Place the slices on a foil-lined and greased
baking tray. Bake at 190°C for about 25 minutes
until the slices are very tender. Arrange the
slices overlapping in a deep dish.

3 Mix together the olive oil, lemon juice or
vinegar, garlic, oregano, pepper and herbs and
pour over the slices. Cover with plastic wrap and
set aside for about 2 hours.

4 If you're not using the eggplant immediately,
store in an airtight container but allow them
to come to room temperature before using.

Top crostini with Roasted Eggplant and tuna – great flavours together – and decorate with a dollop of sour cream with oregano.

Olive Tapenade

This is a basic recipe for tapenade or olive paste. Feel free to add a couple of dried figs to it for variety. Use good quality olives to achieve the best flavour.

1½ cups black olives
56-gram can anchovy fillets
3-4 tblsp capers
1 clove garlic, peeled and crushed
¼ cup olive oil
1 tblsp lemon juice

Put all the ingredients into a food processor and process until smooth.

Cucumber & Chive Mayonnaise

Lovely and delicate, the flavour works very well with artichokes. You really do need a basic homemade mayonnaise for this, as the shop purchased ones end up too thin once the cucumber is added. And the taste is so much better.

Basic Mayonnaise

2 egg yolks
squeeze lemon juice
2 tblsp white wine vinegar
1 tsp Dijon mustard
1 cup olive oil
salt and white pepper

Cucumber and Chives

3 tblsp finely chopped or minced chives
2 tblsp finely chopped basil
¼ cup finely diced or grated cucumber, no seeds or skin
grated rind ½ lemon
1 tsp mustard

1 Beat the egg yolks, lemon juice, vinegar and mustard well with a wooden spoon or in a food processor. Gradually (use a whisk now if making by hand) blend in half the olive oil, drop by drop, so the egg yolks can absorb the oil. Continue in this fashion, only now adding the oil a little faster, until all the oil has been added. The mayonnaise should be thick.

2 Mix the remaining ingredients into the basic mayonnaise and store in the fridge in an airtight container.

Pesto

I cannot imagine summer without pesto. If you can place your hands on loads of basil, it is well worth making this up. Freshly made it is fabulous.

2 cloves garlic, crushed and peeled
50 grams pinenuts (just under ½ cup)
50 grams basil leaves (includes stem weight)
¼ cup grated Italian Parmesan
¾ cup light fruity virgin olive oil

Put the garlic and pinenuts into a food processor and process until chopped finely. Tear the leaves from the basil and discard the stems. Add the Parmesan and basil and, with the motor running, gradually pour the olive oil down the feed tube until the mixture forms a thick paste. Keep in an airtight container.

Variations

- Use walnuts in place of pinenuts.

- For parsley pesto, replace the basil with parsley, preferably Italian parsley, and then add about 6 basil leaves as well.

To Go with Red and White Wines

Rather than begin with the food, here we have started with the wine, and chosen flavours that best suit the different red and white styles.

Simple wine matching

Once you start experimenting with various combinations, it becomes increasingly obvious that some wine and food matches are heavenly and others are horrible.

First let's tackle the things that don't go with wine. Vinegar, unless it is only a dash in a dressing, makes wine taste sour and hard. Egg dishes, where there aren't any other strong flavours, are also difficult to match. Very hot spicy foods will dull the taste of the wine; lager is a better match for these flavours. Very acid fruits like lemon and pineapple are best avoided and chocolate, too, can make wine taste sour.

The first thing to consider when matching wine and food is the flavour intensity of the dish. With strongly flavoured food, a wine with a full, rich flavour is best. With more delicate flavours, choose a lighter more subtle wine style.

STONELEIGH
VINEYARD

MARLBOROUGH
CABERNET

.75cle

Longridge
OF
HAWKES BAY
RNET SAUVIGN
MERLOT
1993
WINE OF NEW ZEALAND

Match the sweetness; sweet wine and sweet food go well together; the wine should be slightly sweeter than the food. Also, match the acidity, acid wines go well with acid food, a good example is tomatoes and Sauvignon Blanc, such as the Stoneleigh Vineyard Marlborough Sauvignon Blanc or the Corbans White Label Gisborne Sauvignon Blanc.

Wine can be chosen to complement the food, or to provide a contrast. For example, venison and mushrooms would be complemented by Cottage Block Pinot Noir, whereas a ripe creamy Brie served with a Stoneleigh Vineyard Marlborough Cabernet Sauvignon would be a contrast.

Salty foods go well with sweet wine, one of the best matches for sweet wine being blue cheese. Oily foods are fine with acid wines; a good match is smoked salmon and sparkling wine, such as Diva or Amadeus Méthode Champenoise.

Try matching the aroma of the wine with a food that has a similar aroma, a good example is Stoneleigh Vineyard Marlborough Cabernet

Sauvignon and roast lamb with mint sauce.

Wine and food matching is not an exact science, it should be fun. Finding exactly the right wine match for your taste is a very pleasurable way of learning more about both food and wine and their flavour components.

WAIMANU
PREMIUM DRY WHITE WINE

Herb Hazelnut Lamb Fillets on French Bread

 Lamb fillets coated with hazelnuts and served warm sliced on French bread are a delicious nibble.

70-gram packet hazelnuts
½ cup soft white
  breadcrumbs
½ cup chopped herbs such
  as parsley, chives,
  thyme, and oregano
1 tblsp olive oil
1 French stick

400 grams lamb
  (about 6 fillets)
2 tblsp each of hazelnut
  and light olive oil
fresh thyme
shredded orange or lemon
  rind
coriander, basil or lettuce

1 Place hazelnuts into a food processor and process until finely ground. Pulse in the breadcrumbs, herbs and oil. Press this mixture over the lamb fillets.

2 Place on a rack in a baking dish. Cook at 200°C for 10 minutes. Cover with tin foil and rest for 10 minutes.

3 Cut the French bread into 1-cm thick slices and toast or grill.

4 Slice lamb on the diagonal. Arrange a piece of herb or lettuce on the bread and top with a slice of lamb.

5 Blend the oils together. Drizzle over a little oil and garnish with thyme and fine shreds of orange or lemon rind.

Makes about 40 pieces

Char-Grilled Venison with Olive & Caper Crumble

Venison is a superb meat; it has a fine texture, is lean and has good flavour. This simple idea can be prepared with beef if you do not have venison, and used to top thick slices of char-grilled bread for your guests to enjoy.

2 cloves garlic, peeled and well mashed

3-4 tblsp virgin olive oil

2 tsp cracked black pepper

350 grams venison steak, preferably thick flank cut

basil leaves (optional)

Olive & Caper Crumble

½ cup black or green olives, pitted

4 sun-dried red peppers or tomatoes, finely sliced

4 tblsp each chopped parsley and marjoram

2 tblsp capers

1 Mix together the garlic, oil and pepper and rub this well into the venison steaks. Set aside to marinate for about 4 hours if you can in a covered container in the fridge.

2 Meanwhile, roughly chop the ingredients for the crumble and set aside.

3 Grill the venison over a high heat allowing 2½-3 minutes on each side. Allow the steaks to stand for 5 minutes before carving into very thin strips.

4 Cut a fresh French bread stick into thick slices. If wished, grill while the venison is standing. Brush with olive oil.

5 Place a whole basil leaf on the base of each bread slice (if using) and arrange a few slices of the venison on top. Garnish with the olive and caper crumble and serve warm.

Makes about 24 pieces

Marinated Rice Filled Grilled Red Peppers

Use short grain rice for this as it holds together better. If you can, prepare these in advance to allow the flavours to marry together. Red peppers are my preference for this, but at Christmas-time you could use green and red!

25 grams butter

½ cup short grain rice

1 cup hot water

2 tblsp olive oil

¼ cup chopped spring onions

1 clove garlic, peeled and crushed

½ small onion, finely chopped

¼ cup chopped parsley

1 tblsp pinenuts, toasted

2 tblsp each minced capers and anchovy fillets

2 tsp lemon juice

6 large red peppers, grilled and peeled (see page 16)

parsley to garnish

Vinaigrette

3 tblsp each good olive oil and red wine vinegar

1 tsp prepared mustard

salt and pepper to season

1 Heat the butter in a saucepan, add the rice and toss well. Pour in the hot water and add a dash of salt. Lower the heat, cover and allow to simmer for about 10-12 minutes until the rice has absorbed all the water and the grains are tender. Set aside.

2 Heat the olive oil in a frying pan and add the spring onions, garlic and onion and cook for about 2 minutes until the onion is tender. Stir in the parsley, chopped pinenuts, capers and anchovies, rice and lemon juice.

3 Cut each pepper in half lengthwise. Place 1-2 tablespoons rice on the pepper and roll up. Place the rolls in a shallow dish as you go. Mix together all the ingredients for the vinaigrette and pour over the rolls. Cover with plastic wrap and refrigerate overnight.

4 Cut the finished peppers in half, to make 24, and place a toothpick through each roll just before serving. Serve the rolls just under room temperature, garnished with Italian parsley.

Makes 24

Chicken Livers in Sherry Sauce

Olives, sherry and chicken make a great combination. Serve these in vol-au-vent cases, and if, like me, you are short on time, buy the cases. Otherwise, use pre-rolled pastry sheets to make your own.

500 grams chicken livers
75 grams butter
3 spring onions, trimmed and chopped
1½ tblsp flour
¾ cup chicken stock
3 tblsp dry sherry
salt and pepper
6 mushrooms, sliced
36 pastry cases
2 tblsp chopped stuffed green olives
2 tblsp finely chopped parsley
2 sun-dried tomatoes in oil, drained and chopped

1 Cut any core part from the livers and then chop them into small pieces.

2 Heat half the butter in a frying pan and when hot add the livers. Brown quickly, but do not cook completely. Remove to a warm platter and season with a little salt.

3 Sauté the spring onions in any remaining butter until they are soft. Add the flour and cook quickly. Add the chicken stock and sherry, and stir constantly until thickened and smooth.

4 Season with salt and pepper and add mushrooms. Simmer covered for 4 minutes. (The mixture can be prepared ahead to this point.) Return livers to the sauce and cook for a couple of minutes.

5 Pile filling into small tartlet cases and decorate with the olives, parsley and sun-dried tomatoes.

Makes 36

Dried Mushrooms in Cream Sauce Pasties

 Using dried mushrooms gives these tasty temptations a real shot of mushroom flavour. I used cèpes.

16 dried mushrooms (either cèpes, morels or shiitake)
½ cup chicken stock
4 tblsp butter
3 shallots, peeled and finely chopped
2 tblsp port
2 tsp double cream
3 sheets pre-rolled puff pastry
beaten egg to glaze

1 Soak the mushrooms in the stock for 30-40 minutes until reconstituted. Strain and reserve the stock.

2 Heat the butter in a frying pan and add the shallots and sauté for 1 minute. Add the mushrooms and sauté for 1 minute.

3 Deglaze the pan with the port and add the reserved soaking liquid and cream. Cook until reduced and thickened and allow to cool.

4 Cut the pastry into 5-6 cm rounds and dampen the edges with a little beaten egg. Place a small amount of filling in the centre. Fold into a semi-circle and press together firmly. Glaze with beaten egg and place onto a greased baking tray. Bake at 220°C for about 10-12 minutes until golden.

Makes about 24

Mini Yorkshires with Rare Roast Beef

I saw this fabulous idea in one of my favourite British magazines, *Good Housekeeping*. So simple, and ideal with a good red wine.

1 cup flour
½ tsp each salt and black pepper
1 tsp English mustard
1 egg
1¼ cups milk
¼ cup finely chopped parsley, preferably Italian
clarified butter or oil

Filling

about 300 grams finely sliced rare roast beef
1 sun-dried red pepper in oil, drained and finely sliced
1 spring onion, trimmed and shredded
1 tblsp horseradish sauce
½ cup sour cream
fresh herbs such as rocket and watercress for garnish

1 In a bowl, sift the flour, salt and pepper. Mix together the mustard, egg, milk and parsley, and then beat into the flour until you reach a smooth batter. Cover and set aside for about 30 minutes.

2 Brush 24 baby muffin tins with melted clarified butter or oil and preheat for 5 minutes in a 240°C oven. Pour in sufficient mixture to come three-quarters the way up each baby muffin tin.

3 Bake at 220°C for 15 minutes or until the Yorkshires are well risen and golden.

4 When cool, hollow out the Yorkshires from underneath and fill with the beef mixture. Garnish with fresh herbs and serve.

Makes 24

Filling

Finely shred the beef and then mix with the red pepper, spring onion, horseradish sauce and sour cream.

Rabbit with Blueberry & Cardamom Chutney

Rabbit slices taken from the fillet, sliced thinly and served on grilled pieces of French bread with a spicy blueberry chutney, make a super change from chicken.

4 rabbit fillets (centre section of rabbit)
2 tblsp olive oil
juice of ½ lemon
1 tsp freshly ground black pepper
1 bay leaf
1-2 loaves fresh French bread
Blueberry & Cardamom Chutney (recipe follows)
herbs to garnish

1 In a bowl, toss together the rabbit, oil, lemon juice, pepper and crushed bayleaf and allow to marinate for 1 hour.

2 Bake at 190°C for 30 minutes or until the rabbit fillets are cooked but not dry. Allow to cool.

3 Slice the rabbit into thin rounds. Cut the French bread into 3-cm thick slices and brush with olive oil.

4 Grill until lightly golden (if you have a barbecue grill, cook them on this).

5 Arrange slices of rabbit on top of a lettuce or herb leaf on the French bread, and add a spoonful of chutney and garnish with fresh herbs.

Makes about 24

Variation

Use chicken or turkey as an alternative to rabbit.

Blueberry & Cardamom Chutney

2 stalks lemon grass, bulb end only
¼ cup olive oil
2 cloves garlic, peeled and finely diced
1 large onion, peeled and diced
2-cm piece fresh ginger, peeled and grated
1 tsp each yellow and brown mustard seeds
¼ tsp each ground coriander and cardamom
1 cup white wine vinegar
1 cup sugar
500 grams blueberries (about 3 punnets)

1 Trim away the reed end of the lemon grass and dice the bulb end finely. Heat the oil in a deep saucepan and add the lemon grass, garlic, onion, ginger and mustard seeds, and cook, stirring, until the mustard seeds have popped. Do not allow the mixture to burn. Add the coriander and cardamom and cook 1 minute more.

2 Add the vinegar and sugar and bring to the boil for 10 minutes.

3 Stir in the blueberries and boil for another 10 minutes. Bottle in hot, sterilised jars and seal. Keep in a cool place.

Makes 2 cups

Pumpkin & Wild Rice Pancakes with Ginger Chicken

Adding wild rice to these pancakes gives them more body and texture. You can leave it out if you wish, or substitute brown rice in its place.

1 cup flour
2 tsp baking powder
½ tsp salt
½ cup puréed pumpkin
1 tsp grated fresh ginger
1 egg
¾ cup milk
½ cup cooked wild rice
knob of butter to pan-fry with

1 Sift the flour, baking powder and salt into a bowl and make a well in the centre.

2 Blend the pumpkin, ginger, egg and milk together and pour into the flour and stir well. Stir in the rice.

3 Heat a knob of butter in a frying pan and cook large tablespoonfuls of the mixture to make pikelet-size pancakes. When the bubbles have risen to the top, turn them over and cook the other side.

4 Stand the cooked pancakes on a wire rack to cool. Cook the remaining mixture.

5 Top each pancake with a little of the Ginger Chicken and serve garnished with fresh herbs.

Makes about 30

Ginger Chicken

1 single chicken breast
3 rashers bacon, trimmed of rind
1 tblsp olive oil
2 tsp minced fresh ginger
3 tblsp each cream cheese and double cream
2 tblsp chopped fresh herbs such as parsley and thyme
salt and pepper

1 Bake the chicken at 180°C for about 30 minutes, or until just cooked. Allow to cool.

2 Shred the bacon into thin strips. Heat the oil in a frying pan and cook the bacon for about 3 minutes, until it becomes fragrant and slightly browned. Stir in the ginger and cook for a further minute.

3 Shred the chicken with a sharp knife, and in a bowl blend the chicken, bacon, cream cheese, cream and herbs together. Season well with salt and pepper.

4 Allow to cool before serving.

Makes about 1 cup

Tarragon Mussels

I'm afraid I'm not a lover of mussels; however they make great nibbles. Mussels have an affinity with tomatoes and fresh parsley.

30-36 medium-sized
   mussels in their shell
4 tomatoes, blanched
½ cup chopped parsley
¼ cup olive oil

2 tblsp tarragon vinegar
1 tblsp lemon juice
black pepper
fresh tarragon to garnish

1 Scrub the mussels well and cut away their beards. Discard any that are open. Put 2 cm of water in a large saucepan and bring to a rapid boil. Add mussels and boil 3-5 minutes until the mussels have opened. Discard any that have not opened. Separate the shells. Remove mussels from shell and keep half of each shell for presentation.

2 Cut the tomatoes in half horizontally. Squeeze out the pulp and discard. Dice the tomato flesh finely. Combine tomato, parsley, oil, vinegar, lemon juice and black pepper. Pour over mussels and place in refrigerator for at least 1 hour to marinate.

3 To serve, place a mussel in each half shell and spoon over a little of the tomato mixture. Garnish with a sprig of tarragon. Serve at room temperature with toothpicks or baby forks.

Makes 30-36

Chicken on Sticks with Walnut Sauce

Chicken is always popular, and the Walnut Sauce will add an interesting contrast.

3 double chicken breasts, skin removed
2 cloves garlic, peeled and crushed
¼ cup lemon juice
¼ cup olive oil

1 Cut the chicken into long strips about 1 cm wide. Combine garlic, lemon juice and oil. Pour over chicken and leave to marinate for at least 1 hour.

2 Thread the chicken in a concertina-fashion onto small satay sticks. Grill or barbecue until cooked. Serve with Walnut Sauce.

Makes about 30

Walnut Sauce

Make sure you have fresh walnuts for this sauce as nuts that are old or off will taint its light taste.

70-gram packet walnut pieces, toasted
1 clove garlic peeled and crushed
¼ cup good olive oil
2 tblsp lemon juice
½ cup natural unsweetened yoghurt
1 tsp honey

1 Place walnuts and garlic in food processor. Process until finely chopped.

2 Add olive oil, lemon juice, yoghurt and honey. Process until smooth.

Cook's Tip

Nuts have a high oil content so keep them in the freezer to stop them going rancid. I tend to roast mine when I get them home and then store them in airtight containers in the freezer.

81

Smoked Chicken Rillettes

Made along the same lines as the Salmon Rillettes, this tasty pâté-style spread is very easy to make. The smoked chicken makes it a little bit more special than just plain chicken, without being too expensive.

¼ cup dry white wine

1½ cups chicken stock

a few parsley and thyme sprigs

1 double chicken breast, skin removed

1 double breast smoked chicken, skin removed

125 grams unsalted butter

1 clove garlic, crushed and peeled

ground black pepper

salt

good dash brandy

1 Put the wine, stock, herbs and chicken into a lidded frying pan and allow to come to the boil. Lower the heat and poach gently for about 15 minutes, turning once until the chicken is just cooked. Remove from the poaching liquid, cover with plastic wrap and allow to cool.

2 Tear the smoked chicken into small pieces. Heat 25 grams of the butter in a frying pan and add the smoked chicken and the garlic and cook over a moderate heat for about 5 minutes. Remove from the pan and cool.

3 Place the smoked chicken, chicken and remaining butter in a food processor and pulse until the mixture is just blended but with texture. Season with pepper, salt and a good dash of brandy.

4 Serve at room temperature on slices of crusty bread, such as ciabatta, and top with fine slices of sun-dried red pepper in oil or tomatoes and fresh herbs.

Makes 1 1/2 cups

Chicken Wing Nibbles

Chicken wings make fabulous nibbles. Purchased in packs from the supermarket, they are easy to use and there are heaps of possibilities. Trim away the tip end (and if you are into making homemade stock you will be able to use these rather than just throwing them away). Cut the wings between the joint to make two pieces and you are away.

Cajun Nibbles

This recipe makes good use of the pre-made seasonings from famous Louisiana chef, Paul Prudhomme. You can just dust the wings with the 'Magic' and grill. I have added a little wine for more good taste. The spicy sauce that accompanies them can be made in advance, but needs a good whizzing before being served.

1 kg chicken wings, prepared as above
3 tblsp Paul Prudhomme's Poultry Magic
½ cup white wine

Spicy Sauce

6 spring onions, trimmed
2 cloves garlic, crushed and peeled
2-cm piece root ginger, peeled
1 tblsp brown sugar
1 orange, peeled to remove rind and skin
1 tsp each ground allspice, white pepper and cinnamon
½ tsp each ground nutmeg and cayenne
2 tblsp chopped fresh thyme
½ cup each freshly squeezed orange juice and white wine vinegar
2 tblsp dark soy sauce or Indonesian Ketjap Manis
2 tblsp olive oil

1 Mix the Poultry Magic and wine together in a lidded container and toss in the chicken wings. Cover and marinate overnight or for about 4 hours.

2 Heat the fan grill to about 200°C (if you do not have a fan grill, heat the grill to 220°C). Arrange the chicken nibbles on a rack and grill for about 15 minutes or until golden. Turn occasionally during cooking.

3 Serve in a large basket with the spicy sauce.

Makes about 20

Spicy Sauce

Put all the ingredients except the oil into a food processor and process until the mixture is well blended. With the motor running, pour the oil down the feed tube until it is well mixed in. This sauce is particularly nice when first made.

Indonesian Chicken Nibbles

Using pre-packaged spices does help when you are in a hurry. I devised this recipe one night when we were having unexpected guests in for drinks and I happened to have a packet of Ma Healion's Bahme Goreng mix on hand.

1 kg chicken wings, prepared as above
about ¾ cup seasoned flour
1 egg
½ cup milk
75-gram packet Ma Healion's Bahme Goreng mix
1 cup dry white breadcrumbs
oil to deep-fry

Sauce

second sachet from Ma Healion's mix
½ cup water
¼ cup each cream and non-fat plain yoghurt
2 tblsp honey

1 Put the seasoned flour into a bag then toss the chicken wings in the flour.

2 Beat the egg and milk together in a deep bowl. Mix 1 sachet from the Ma Healion's Bahme Goreng mix with the white breadcrumbs and place this mixture in a plastic bag or on a plate.

3 Coat the chicken wings in the egg mixture and then toss in the breadcrumb mix. Place on a plate in one layer.

4 Heat the oil to 180°C and deep-fry the chicken wings for about 7-8 minutes, until they are deep golden and cooked. It is wise with this recipe to take one chicken wing out to check that they are thoroughly cooked.

5 Drain wings on absorbent paper and then pile into a large basket and serve with the dipping sauce.

Makes about 20

Dipping sauce

Put the contents of the second sachet from Ma Healion's packet into a saucepan and stir in the water. Bring to the boil and simmer for about 3 minutes. Stir in the cream, yoghurt and honey. Serve warm.

Cook's Tip

You can also bake these nibbles at 200°C for about 15 minutes or until cooked.

Spiced New Potatoes with Roasted Garlic Dressing

Sweet new potatoes are so welcomed when they arrive. Hand them out, either warm or cold, on a large platter.

600 grams medium-sized new potatoes, scrubbed
2 tblsp clarified butter
2 tsp garam masala
1/2 tsp lemon rind
1/2 tsp salt
1/2 tsp pepper

1 Cook the potatoes. Cool, drain and cut larger ones in half.

2 Heat clarified butter in large pan. Add garam masala, lemon rind, salt and pepper. Add potatoes and cook over medium heat, tossing until the potatoes are slightly browned and well flavoured.

3 Serve warm or cold with Roasted Garlic Dressing and plenty of skewers.

Roasted Garlic Dressing

1 bulb garlic
250 grams light sour cream
1/4 tsp salt
2 tblsp each chopped chives and parsley

1 Wrap garlic bulb in tin foil and bake at 180°C for 1 hour, or until well cooked. Cool.

2 Cut the garlic bulb in half horizontally and squeeze the pulp into a food processor. Add the sour cream and salt and process until smooth. Pulse in the chives and parsley.

Corbans Estate Varietals

Building on a history of quality wines since 1902, Corbans has just released

a new range of four single varietal wines which are excellent value for money. There are two wines from Gisborne – a Chardonnay and a Sauvignon Blanc – and two wines from Marlborough – a Riesling and a Gewurztraminer. The wines in this range are of excellent quality, consistent with Corbans' medal-winning heritage. All of the wines in the Corbans Estate range are ideal food wines and great value for everyday.

Robard & Butler Range

Based on the concept of a French wine negociant, Robard & Butler has built a solid reputation for offering good wines at a fair price. Within the range are a number of local and imported wines, including Chardonnay Méthode Champenoise, South East Australian Cabernet

Shiraz and Chardonnay. There is always something new and special in the range to ensure wine-lovers a few surprises!

Longridge of Hawkes Bay Range

A leading boutique winemaker, Longridge of Hawkes Bay offers a range of premium varietal wines from three vineyards – Omaranui, Tuki Tuki and Haumoana – which are situated about ten kilometres south of Napier. The specific geography of the region, with its sheltered valleys and high sunshine hours, produces the superior grapes used in making these premium wines. Longridge of Hawkes Bay offers a range of premium

varietals – Chardonnay, Sauvignon Blanc Oak Aged, Gewurztraminer (a trophy winner for the best wine in that style at a recent national wine awards) and Cabernet Sauvignon.

Stoneleigh Vineyard Marlborough Range

Situated on the plains of the Wairau River in Marlborough, the Stoneleigh Vineyard derives its name from the 'stony paddocks' of the region. The river plains, with their free-draining stony soils and layers of moisture-retaining silt, contribute to the

exceptional quality of Stoneleigh wines. Since they were launched in 1986, Stoneleigh wines have had outstanding medal successes in both international and domestic wine competitions. More than 100 medals – including 15 gold medals – have been won. The Stoneleigh range includes Sauvignon Blanc, Chardonnay, Rhine Riesling and Cabernet Sauvignon.

Corbans Private Bin Range

Corbans Private Bin is a range of flagship premium varietals selected from New Zealand's premier wine-growing regions. Each wine is chosen as an excellent example of the wine styles that prosper within those regions. For example, Chardonnays from Gisborne and Marlborough, Rhine Riesling from Amberley, Sauvignon Blanc from Marlborough

and Cabernet Sauvignon from Hawkes Bay. The Corbans Private Bin range has a strong heritage of medal success, including New Zealand's ultimate accolade for outstanding quality – the champion wine of the show at the national wine awards. Wine-lovers recognise this range for its quality.

Corbans Amadeus Méthode Champenoise

Amadeus is a premium New Zealand Méthode Champenoise. It is made from a blend of Pinot Noir and Chardonnay grapes grown in Hawkes Bay. The wine is bottle-fermented, with each bottle handturned in the traditional manner of Champagne-style wines. With the benefit of three years of bottle ageing, Amadeus has a light and elegant, crisp yeasty nose and fine bead. It has achieved significant medal success and is an excellent example of this wine style.

Cooks Winemakers Reserve Range

The Cooks Winemakers Reserve range features premium varietals which have been sourced historically

from Hawkes Bay. The Chardonnay is perhaps the most famous wine from the range, with a strong history of gold medal success dating back to the early 1980s.

Index